# Norris on Trout Fishing

*Thaddeus Norris, courtesy of the American Museum of Fly Fishing, Manchester, Vermont*

# Norris on Trout Fishing

A LIFETIME OF ANGLING
INSIGHTS

*Selected and introduced
by Paul Schullery*

STACKPOLE
BOOKS

Introductions and back matter copyright © 2008 by Paul Schullery

Published by
STACKPOLE BOOKS
5067 Ritter Road
Mechanicsburg, PA 17055
www.stackpolebooks.com

All rights reserved, including the right to reproduce this book or portions thereof in any form or by any means, electronic or mechanical, including photocopying, recording, or by any information storage and retrieval system, without permission in writing from the publisher. All inquiries should be addressed to Stackpole Books, 5067 Ritter Road, Mechanicsburg, Pennsylvania 17055.

Printed in the United States

First edition

10 9 8 7 6 5 4 3 2 1

Illustrations for chapters 1, 2, 3, 5, and 6 are from Thaddeus Norris, *The American Angler's Book* (1864). Illustrations for chapter four are from Alfred M. Mayer, *Sport with Rod and Gun* (1883). New and extended captions have been provided for a number of the illustrations.

**Library of Congress Cataloging-in-Publication Data**

Norris, Thaddeus, 1811–1877.
  Norris on trout fishing : a lifetime of angling insights / selected and introduced by Paul Schullery.—1st ed.
    p. cm.
  Includes bibliographical references.
  ISBN-13: 978-0-8117-0351-2 (hardcover)
  ISBN-10: 0-8117-0351-7 (hardcover)
 1. Trout fishing—Anecdotes. 2. Fly fishing—Anecdotes. 3. Norris, Thaddeus, 1811–1877. I. Schullery, Paul. II. Title.

SH687.N67 2008
799.17157—dc22

2007036712

# SERIES INTRODUCTION

We fly fishers are rightly proud of our long and distinguished literary tradition, but too much of that tradition has slipped out of reach. It is unfortunate enough that most of the older books are unobtainable, but as the sport's techniques, language, and even values change, the older authors become less accessible to us even when we do read them. Fly fishing's great old stories and wisdoms are often concealed in unfamiliar prose styles, extinct tackle terminology, and abandoned jargon.

The lessons and excitement of these older works will only survive if we keep reading them. By presenting the most readily accessible material from these authors, this series invites you to explore the rest of their work. Whether the selections in each book are instructive, entertaining, or inspirational, it is our fondest hope that they will whet your appetite for more of this lovely sport's literary adventures.

It is one of fly fishing's greatest attractions that the actual fishing is accompanied by a vast and endlessly engaging conversation. We have been conducting this conversation in print for many centuries now, and we seem always to have more to say. In this series, we invite you to sit back, turn the page, and give a listen. The conversation has never been better.

Paul Schullery
Series editor

# CONTENTS

| | |
|---|---:|
| *Introduction.* | viii |
| **One:** Angling. | 1 |
| **Two:** Brook Trout. Speckled Trout. | 16 |
| **Three:** Trout Fly-Fishing.—The Stream. | 34 |
| **Four:** The Michigan Grayling. | 61 |
| **Five:** Fly-Fishing Alone. | 82 |
| **Six:** The Great Lake Trout. | 112 |
| **Seven:** A Note on Fly Theory. | 116 |
| *Additional readings on Thaddeus Norris.* | 118 |
| *Sources of the chapters.* | 119 |

# INTRODUCTION

Thaddeus Norris (1811–1877) occupies a position of extraordinary significance in American fishing history. In the early 1800s, the first American angling journalists borrowed heavily from British sources, for both their natural history and their fishing techniques. But with Norris's monumental *The American Angler's Book* (1864), we firmly declared, if not our independence of the British experts, at least our confidence in our own observations and experiences. Arnold Gingrich, one of modern fly fishing's most literate commentators, described Norris as "the cornerstone of American angling literature."

Norris brought an amazing breadth of knowledge to his work, including familiarity with all the important native fishes of eastern North America and an equally broad familiarity with the many ways in which they might be captured with hook and line. His lifetime bridged the period when Americans went from having essentially no tackle industry to making some of the finest rods, reels, and flies in the world. Norris was one of American tackle-making's pioneers and here too he displayed special gifts.

But for all this technical expertise, it was his companionable nature and literary style that most set him above other nineteenth-century experts. He was known almost universally as "Uncle Thad," and in that eventful stretch of decades bracketed by the Civil War and World War I—from Abraham Lincoln to Woodrow Wilson—there was no more widely admired authority on American angling. Norris was, and should still be, read as much for the good company he provides as for his angling wisdom.

Some writers have tried to capture the essence of his popularity by describing him as "the American Walton." It's a nice compliment, but it doesn't really work. Walton himself was everybody's Walton, including ours. Norris didn't have to be the American Walton because he was the American Norris. As angling historian Charles Goodspeed put it in 1939, "in a sport where discoveries in the realm of practice as well as improvements in tackle are continually being made any book will naturally become obsolete as a practical manual in seventy-five years, 'Thad Norris' still commands the gratitude, admiration, and even affection of his readers, who find therein the self-portrait of a lovable man." As we approach the sesquicentenary of his book, it's a good time to read him again, partly for the fun of what he had to say and partly to remember how it was when Norris was astream.

Norris loved many kinds of fishing, but trout were nearest his heart. For this new sampler of his writings I've chosen a combination of his practical advice and his philosophical ruminations, hoping to capture both sides of this friendliest of experts. I've included excerpts from *The American Angler's Book* that display his gifts for natural history, practical instruction, and philosophical deliberation. To those I've added an account he wrote a few years later (just before his death) of his experiences on a few trips to the grayling rivers of the Michigan wilderness—a story that combines the excitement of pioneering a new sporting field with our own melancholy hindsight that within a few short decades of Norris's own death this beautiful species would also be gone, destroyed by overfishing and habitat destruction.

But before turning to his writings, it's worth a brief moment's preparation. Norris wrote long ago,

## Introduction

and we write, think, and fish somewhat differently now.

I suspect that for most of us today, the biggest shock in reading Norris will come as he starts to kill fish; he and his companions routinely killed far more trout than we would consider acceptable today. The fly-fishing sensibility has changed much since his time and, as smart as he was, Norris was still a man of his times. On the other hand, he was at the forefront of changing definitions of sportsmanship in those times, and it is some indication of his relative enlightenment that he believed that the "truehearted" angler released most of his catch. He believed and preached this at a time when almost all his contemporaries killed everything they could get—all sizes, all species, all the time.

Modern readers may also stumble over some terminology, especially in tackle. Norris fished with silkworm gut leaders, so when he mentions "gut" just read "leader." He also fished before split bamboo rods took over the sport, so his rods were solid wood, typically twelve feet long for trout (imagine casting such a thing, one-handed, through a long day of fishing, and your respect for his crowd can only increase). As late as the Civil War, when his big book was published, ferrules were so unreliable that these hefty rods were often rigged with small wire hooks on both sides the ferrule joint so that the angler could lash the joint together with thread in case the ferrule failed.

The attentive reader will also find some minor factual complications here and there. Our exploration of our fisheries was still incomplete in his day; Norris thought the brook trout did not live south of Virginia when it was native to the Blue Ridge well south of that through the Great Smoky Mountains. He referred to the native trout of the American West and Pacific Coast as brook trout, when we now appreciate a host of other native trout in those immense regions (also, the term "brook trout" was often informally applied to western trouts for many years; it meant not just Brook Trout, as a species, but brook trout, as fish that live in brooks), and his awareness of the distribution of grayling in the American West was incomplete and erroneous. He almost certainly overestimated the destructiveness of most Native American trout fishers.

There is also a certain amount of "insider" talk, just as there is in today's fishing writing. For example, Norris's mentions of the "Houseless" is just a reference to an informal little group of angling friends who, because they chose not to have an official club-

## Introduction

house—and therefore also chose to be primarily a true fishing club rather than a social club—referred to themselves as the "Houseless Anglers."

These differences between us and him, and his occasional factual lapse or uncertainty of information, are trivial matters in the big picture of what Norris has to tell us. We don't read Norris now for tackle tips or taxonomy anyway. We read him for the greater illuminations found in hearing from any great angling thinker, and in the greater joys of his storytelling.

Norris lived in an age of genuine angling discovery. His observations on the use of floating flies, on the pros and cons of various imitative theories, and on the best ways to manipulate multiple-fly casts are all intriguing even today, but when I say discovery I mean real discovery. There were still countless North American waters, especially in the West, that had never seen a fly, just as there were still many puzzles to be sorted out in the identities of native fish. Through his tales we can share not only the fabulous fishing but the sense of exploration and adventure that accompanied it.

When we read Norris, we reach back into a lost age in American angling. Norris left the American angling scene just as things were about to get a great deal more complicated because of the wholesale translocation of native fish to countless new waters and the momentous arrival of European trout in just as many American waters. He fished in a very different America, one we would do well to think about now and then.

At the same time, we can listen in on some great talk. His literary conversation with his British forebears and his American counterparts is a wonderful commentary on the hows and whys of fishing, not just in his day but in any day. If you're new to fishing literature, Norris's references to this or that author should serve as a recommendation for a lot more fascinating reading.

For Norris, as for most of us when we fish, moments of excitement alternated with reveries on the fish, the grand theatre of nature that surrounds the river, and even on why we anglers are such a diverse, peculiar, and endlessly amusing crowd. In 1883, Fred Mather, the eminent American fish culturist and angling writer (at a time when a person could still be both), predicted that "In another century Norris will be more read and appreciated than he is to-day. Of all American angling writers of this century he will stand foremost. . . ." Mather was right in principle—Norris deserves to be read by

## Introduction

every generation, much as Walton does—but wrong in fact. Hardly any modern American anglers read Norris, Mather, and their friends today. I hope that this little book will help to change that.

Paul Schullery

# CHAPTER ONE

# *Angling.*

*It's harmonizing influences.—Recollections of Angling in boyhood, its after influence on manhood.—Its social tendency.—What and Who is an Angler?—Different kinds of Anglers.—The Snob Angler.—The Greedy Angler.—The Spick-and-Span Angler.—The Rough-and-Ready Angler.—The Literary Angler.—The Shad-roe Fisherman.—The English Admiral, an Angler.—The True Angler.*

It is not my intention to offer any remarks on the antiquity of Angling, or say much in its defence. Dame Juliana Berners, Isaac Walton, and more recent authors, have discoursed learnedly on its origin, and defended it wisely and valiantly from the aspersions and ridicule of those who cannot appreciate its quiet joys, and who know not the solace and peace it brings to the harassed mind, or how it begets and fosters contentment and a love of nature.

I ask any caviller to read Dr. Bethune's Bibliographical Preface to his edition of Walton; and then

Father Izaak's address to the readers of his discourse, "but especially to THE HONEST ANGLER," and accompany him in spirit, as Bethune does, by the quiet Lea, or Cotton by the bright rippling Dove; and if he be not convinced of the blessed influences of the "gentle art," or if his heart is not warmed, or no recollections of his boyish days come back to him, I give him up without a harsh word, but with a feeling of regret, that a lifetime should be spent without attaining so much of quiet happiness that might have been so easily possessed, and quoting a few sad words from Whittier's Maud Muller, I only say "it might have been."

Many anglers, such as Sir Humphrey Davy and Sir Joshua Reynolds, besides some of my own acquaintance, have sought its cheering influences in advanced life. I know of one whose early manhood and maturer years were spent on the boisterous deep, and who, though now past eighty, is still an ardent, but quiet angler: and when no better sport can be found, he will even fish through the ice in winter for Roach. No doubt his days have been lengthened out, and the burden of life lightened, by his love of angling.

But how sweetly memories of the past come to one who has appreciated and enjoyed it from his

## Angling.

boyhood, whose almost first penny, after he wore jacket and trowsers, bought his first fish-hook; whose first fishing-line was twisted by mother or sister; whose float was the cork of a physic vial, and whose sinkers were cut from the sheet-lead of an old tea-chest! Thus rigged, with what glad anticipations of sport, many a boy has started on some bright Saturday morning, his gourd, or old cow's horn of red worms in one pocket, and a jack-knife in the other, to cut his alder-pole with, and wandered "free and far" by still pool and swift waters, dinnerless—except perhaps a slight meal at a cherry tree, or a handful of berries that grew along his path—and come home at night weary and footsore, but exulting in his string of chubs, minnows, and sunnies, the largest as broad as his three fingers! He almost falls asleep under his Saturday night scrubbing, but in the morning, does ample justice to his "catch," which is turned out of the pan, crisp and brown, and matted together like a pan-cake.

In *my* school days, a boy might have been envied, but not loved for proficiency in his studies; but *he* was most courted, who knew the best fishing-holes; who had plenty of powder and shot; the best squirrel dog, and the use of his father's long flintlock gun. And I confess, as I write these lines with my spectacles on, that I have still a strong drawing towards this type of a boy, whether I meet him in my lonely rambles, or whether he dwells only in my memory.

Sometimes the recollection of our boyish sports comes back to us after manhood, and one who has been "addicted" to fishing relapses into his old "ailment;" then angling becomes a pleasant kind of disease, and one's friends are apt to become inoculated with the virus, for it is contagious. Or men are informally introduced to each other on the stream, by a good-humored salutation, or an inquiry of *"What luck?"* or a display of the catch, or the offer of a segar, or the flask, or a new fly; and with such introduction have become fast friends, from that affinity which draws all true anglers together.

But let me ask what is an angler, and who is a *true* angler? One who fishes with nets is not, neither is he who spears, snares, or dastardly uses the crazy bait to *get* fish, or who catches them on set lines; nor is he who is boisterous, noisy, or quarrelsome; nor are those who profess to practise the higher branches of the art, and affect contempt for their more humble brethren, who have not attained to *their* proficiency, imbued with the feeling that should possess the true angler.

Nor is he who brings his ice-chest from town, and fishes all day with worm or fly, that he may

*Angling.*

return to the city and boastingly distribute his soaked and tasteless trout among his friends, and brag of the numbers he has basketed, from fingerlings upwards.

Anglers may be divided into almost as many genera and species as the fish they catch, and engage in the sport from as many impulses. Let me give, "en passant," a sketch of a few of the many I have met with.

There is the Fussy Angler, a great bore; of course you will shun him. The "Snob" Angler, who speaks confidently and knowingly on a slight capital of skill or experience. The Greedy, Pushing Angler, who rushes ahead and half fishes the water, leaving those who follow, in doubt as to whether he has fished a pool or rift carefully, or slurred it over in his haste to reach some well known place down the stream before his companions. The company of these, the quiet, careful angler will avoid.

We also meet sometimes with the "Spick-and-Span" Angler, who has a highly varnished rod, and a superabundance of useless tackle; his outfit is of the most elaborate kind as regards its finish. He is a dapper "well got up" angler in all his appointments, and fishes much in-doors over his claret and poteen, when he has a good listener. He frequently displays bad taste in his tackle, intended for fly-fishing, by having a thirty dollar multiplying reel, filled with one of Conroy's very best relaid sea-grass lines, strong enough to hold a dolphin. If you meet him on the teeming waters of northern New York, the evening's display of his catch, depends much on the rough skill of his guide.

The Rough-and-Ready Angler, the opposite of the afore-named, disdains all "tomfoolery," and carries his tackle in an old shot-bag, and his flies in a tangled mass.

*Angling.*

We have also the Literary Angler, who reads Walton and admires him hugely; he has been inoculated with the *sentiment* only; the five-mile walk up the creek, where it has not been fished much, is very fatiguing to him; he "did not know he must wade the stream," and does not until he slips in, and then he has some trouble at night to get his boots off. He is provided with a stout bass rod, good *strong* leaders of salmon-gut, and a stock of Conroy's "journal flies," and wonders if he had not better put on a *shot* just above his stretcher-fly.

The Pretentious Angler, to use a favorite expression of the lamented Dickey Riker, once Recorder of the city of New York, is one "that prevails to a great extent in this community." This gentleman has many of the qualities attributed by Fisher, of the "Angler's Souvenir," to Sir Humphrey Davy. If he has attained the higher branches of the art, he affects to despise all sport which he considers less scientific; if a salmon fisher, he calls trout "vermin;" if he is a trout fly-fisher, he professes contempt for bait fishing. We have talked with true anglers who were even disposed to censure the eminent Divine, who has so ably, and with such labor of love, edited our American edition of Walton, for affectation, in saying of the red worm, "our hands have long since been washed of the dirty things." The servant should not be above his master, and certainly "Iz. Wa.," whose disciple the Doctor professed to be, considered it no indignity to use them, nor was he disgusted with his "horn of gentles." But the Doctor was certainly right in deprecating the use of ground bait in reference to trout, when the angler can with a little faith and less greed soon learn the use of the fly.

The *Shad-roe Fisherman.*—The habitat of this genus (and they are rarely found elsewhere) is Philadelphia. There are many persons of the aforesaid city, who fish only when this bait can be had, and an idea seems to possess them that fish will bite at no other. This fraternity could have been found some years back, singly or in pairs, or little coteries of three or four, on any sun-shiny day from Easter to Whitsuntide, heaving their heavy dipsies and horsehair snoods from the ends of the piers, or from canal-boats laid up in ordinary—the old floating bridge at Gray's Ferry was a favorite resort for them. Sometimes the party was convivial, and provided with a junk bottle of what they believed to be *old rye.*

Before the gas-works had destroyed the fishing in the Schuylkill, I frequently observed a solitary individual of this species, wending his way to the river on

Sunday mornings, with a long reed-pole on his shoulder, and in his hand a tin kettle of shad-roe; and his "prog," consisting of hard-boiled eggs and crackers and cheese, tied up in a cotton bandana handkerchief. Towards nightfall "he might have been seen" (as James the novelist says of the horseman), trudging home-ward with a string of Pan Rock and White Perch, or "Catties" and Eels, his trowsers and coat sleeves well plastered with his unctuous bait, suggesting the idea of what, in vulgar parlance, might be called "a very nasty man."

But let us not turn up our scientific noses at this humble brother; nor let the home missionary or tract distributor rate him too severely, if he should meet with him in his Sunday walks; for who can tell what a quiet day of consolation it has been to him; he has found relief from the toils and cares of the week, and perhaps from the ceaseless tongue of his shrewish "old woman." If his sport has been good, he follows it up the next day, and keeps "blue Monday."

We have seen some very respectable gentlemen in our day engaged in fishing with shad-roe at Fairmount Dam. The bar even had its representative, in one of our first criminal court lawyers. He did not "dress the character" with as much discrimination as when he lectured on Shakespeare, for he always wore his blue coat with gilt buttons: he did not appear to be a successful angler. "Per contra" to this was a wealthy retired merchant, who used to astonish us with his knack of keeping this difficult bait on his hooks, and his skill in hooking little White Perch. Many a troller has seen him sitting bolt upright in the bow of his boat on a cool morning in May, with his overcoat buttoned up to his chin, his jolly spouse in the stern, and his servant amidship, baiting the hooks and taking off the lady's fish. The son also was an adept as well as the sire. Woe to the perch fisher, with his bait of little silvery eels, if these occupied the lower part of the swim, for the fish were all arrested by the stray ova that floated off from the "gobs" of shad-roe.

As we love contrasts, let us here make a slight allusion to that sensible "old English gentleman," the Admiral, who surveyed the north-west coast of America, to see, if in the contingency of the Yankees adhering to their claim of "fifty-four forty," the country about Vancouver's Island was worth contending for. He was an ardent angler, and it is reported, that on leaving his ship he provided stores for a week, which comprised of course not a few drinkables, as well as salmon rods and other tackle, and started in his boats to explore the rivers and tributaries, which, so goes the story, were so crammed in many places with salmon, that they could be captured with a boat-hook; and still with all the variety of salmon flies and the piscatory skill of the admiral and his officers, not a fish could be induced to rise at the fly. He returned to his ship disheartened and disgusted, averring that the country was not worth contending for; that the Yankees might have it and be ———; but it would be indecorous to record the admiral's mild expletive.

The *True Angler* is thoroughly imbued with the spirit of gentle old Izaak. He has no affectation, and when a fly-cast is not to be had, can find amusement in catching Sunfish or Roach, and does not despise the sport of any humbler brother of the angle. With him, fishing is a recreation, and a "calmer of unquiet thoughts." He never quarrels with his luck, knowing that satiety dulls one's appreciation of sport as much as want of success, but is ever content when he has done his best, and looks hopefully forward to a more propitious day. Whether from boat or rocky shore, or along the sedgy bank of the creek, or the stony margin of the mountain brook, he deems it an achievement to take fish when they are difficult to catch, and his satisfaction is in proportion. If he is lazy, or a superannuated angler, he can even endure a few days' trolling on an inland lake, and smokes his cigar, chats with the boatman, and takes an occasional "nip" as he is rowed along the wooded shore and amongst the beautiful islands.

A true angler is generally a modest man; unobtrusively communicative when he can impart a new idea; and is ever ready to let a pretentious tyro have his say, and good-naturedly (as if merely suggesting how it should be done) repairs his tackle, or gets him out of a scrape. He is moderately provided with all tackle and "fixins" necessary to the fishing he is in pursuit of. Is quietly self-reliant and equal to almost any emergency, from splicing his rod or tying his own flies, to trudging ten miles across a rough country with his luggage on his back. His enjoyment consists not only in the taking of fish: he draws much pleasure from the soothing influence and delightful accompaniments of the art.

With happy memories of the past summer, he joins together the three pieces of his fly-rod at home, when the scenes of the last season's sport are wrapped in snow and ice, and renews the glad feelings of long summer days. With what interest he notes the swelling of the buds on the maples, or the advent of the blue-bird and robin, and looks forward to the day when he is to try another cast! and, when it comes at last, with what pleasing anticipations he packs up his "traps," and leaves his business cares and the noisy city behind, and after a few hours' or few days' travel in the cars, and a few miles in a rough wagon, or a vigorous tramp over rugged hills or along the road that leads up the banks of the river, he arrives at his quarters! He is now in the region of fresh butter and mealy potatoes—there are always good potatoes in a mountainous trout country. How pleasingly rough everything looks after leaving the prim city! How pure and wholesome the air! How beautiful the clumps of sugar-maples and the veteran hemlocks jutting out over the stream; the laurel; the ivy; the moss-covered rocks; the lengthening shadows of evening! How musical the old familiar tinkling of the cow-bell and the cry of the whip-poor-will! How sweetly he is lulled to sleep as he hears

> "The waters leap and gush
> O'er channelled rock, and broken bush!"

Next morning, after a hearty breakfast of mashed potatoes, ham and eggs, and butter from the cream of the cow that browses in the woods, he is off, three miles up the creek, a cigar or his pipe in his mouth, his creel at his side, and his rod over his shoulder, chatting with his chum as he goes; free, joyous, happy; at peace with his Maker, with himself, and all mankind; he should be grateful for this much, even if he catches no fish. How exhilarating the music of the stream! how invigorating its waters, causing a consciousness of manly vigor, as he wades sturdily with the strong current and casts his flies before him! When his zeal abates, and a few of the *speckled* lie in the bottom of his creel, he is not less interested in the wild flowers on the bank, or the scathed old hemlock on the cliff above, with its hawk's nest, the lady of the house likely inside, and the male proprietor perched high above on its dead top, and he breaks forth lustily—the scene suggesting the song—

"The bee's on its wing, and the hawk on its nest,
And the river runs merrily by."

When noon comes on, and the trout rise lazily or merely nip, he halts "sub tegmine fagi," or under the shadow of the dark sugar-maple to build a fire and roast trout for his dinner, and wiles away three hours or so. He dines sumptuously, straightens and dries his leader and the gut of his dropper, and repairs all breakage. He smokes leisurely, or even takes a nap on the green sward or velvety moss, and resumes his

*Angling.*

sport when the sun has declined enough to shade at least one side of the stream, and pleasantly anticipates the late evening cast on the still waters far down the creek. God be with you, gentle angler, if actuated with the feeling of our old master! whether you are a top fisher or a bottom fisher; whether your bait be gentles, brandling, grub, or red worm; crab, shrimp, or minnow; caddis, grasshopper, or the feathery counterfeit of the ephemera. May your thoughts be always peaceful, and your heart filled with gratitude to Him who made the country and the rivers; and "may the east wind never blow when you go a fishing!"

# CHAPTER TWO

# *Brook Trout.*
# *Speckled Trout.*

*Salmo fontinalis:* Mitchil.

Form elliptical, elongated. Color, olive on the back, shading gradually lighter to the lateral line; sides still lighter, with roseate pearly reflections; belly white and rose-tinted, sometimes shaded with yellow, and occasionally a deep orange. The markings of this fish are beautiful; the sides are covered with yellowish spots of metallic lustre interspersed above and below the lateral line with smaller spots of bright vermilion; the back is vermiculated, that is, marked with dark tracings of irregular form, many of which run into each other. The dorsal fin has five or six lines of dark spots; the pectorals are olive, with the exception of the two anterior rays, which are black and much stouter than the others; the anterior ray of the ventrals and anal is white, the next black, and the remaining rays a

*Brook Trout. Speckled Trout.*

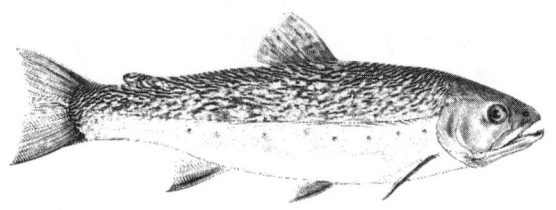

*The Brook Trout*

deep orange; the caudal is slightly concave, with dusky markings on the upper border of the rays. The head is rather more than one-fifth the length of the body, exclusive of caudal; breadth one-fourth.

There are ten branchial rays: the first dorsal fin has eleven rays; the second dorsal being adipose is without rays; the pectorals have twelve rays; the ventrals eight; anal nine; caudal nineteen.

No fish affords as much sport to the angler as the Brook Trout; whether he is fished for by the country urchin, who ties his knotted horsehair-line to his alder-pole, and "snakes out" the speckled fellows by the caving-bank of the meadow brook, and from under the overhanging branches of the wooded stream; or by the scientific angler, who delivers his flies attached to his nine-foot leader—straight out and lightly—from his well-balanced rod, and kills his fish artistically.

He is as game as a bantam cock, and with a pliant rod and fine tackle, a twelve-incher gives as much sport as most other fish of four times his size, on a stout rod and coarse tackle. But let us begin with a slight glance at his habits and natural history; his unnatural death we will speak of afterwards; though the angler may think it more natural that the Trout should die by his hands, than in any other way.

Towards the end of August, if you loiter along a Trout stream, and look into a pool with smooth gliding current, where a spring branch enters; or wander along the banks of some clear, cool tributary of the main brook, you may find a dozen Trout congregated—sometimes a half dozen or a single pair—and if not disturbed by a freshet, caught by the angler, or snared by the villanous poacher, with his wire-loop, they will remain there until October or November, when the female will cast her spawn—some say in a furrow, made longitudinally or diagonally in the bed of the stream, by rooting with her nose; others say, more after the manner of broadcast. Whichever it be, the male fish follows immediately, ejecting his milt over it. The parents of the future progeny then, as a usual thing, take their course down stream to some deep pool, and there remain in winter quarters, recovering strength and flesh until the ensuing spring, when they move up stream with every rise of water, always on the lookout for something to eat, and ever eager to take a bait or rise at a fly, and reproducing in autumn as before.

After fecundation the ova assumes a somewhat brownish transparent hue, each egg showing in its centre a small dark spot, which is the embryo of the future fish. The young fish are hatched out in two or three months, and appear somewhat larger than the little wriggle-tails in a barrel of stale rainwater. They have large prominent eyes and little pot-bellies, ichthyologically termed "umbilical bladders," in which is stored the sustenance left from the egg, and which lasts three or four weeks, or until they commence seeking their own food. By this time they have grown to an inch and a half long; they then seek the shallows and gentle margins of the brook, or smaller rills, and commence feeding on minute aquatic insects and the larva of flies.

It is surprising how small a quantity of running water will sustain a school of young Trout. I have seen a half dozen in a track left by a horse's foot, in a mossy spring branch. Trout have the same dusky patches or finger-marks, that all their congeners have, when young. As far as I have observed, they rarely attain a size beyond four or five inches during the first summer in our mountain streams. They seldom venture into the larger waters until the second summer, when they are the little fingerlings that jump at one's droppers, as he is killing their progenitor on the stretcher-fly.

At our noonings, when we have emptied our creels to select the larger fish for a roast, or a bake under the ashes, I have placed the whole catch in a row, the smallest at one end, increasing in size to the largest at the other end, and endeavored to theorize as to their ages, or separate the yearlings from the two year old, and those of three from those of four years; but have never been able to draw a line separating, with any degree of certainty, the fish of a year from those of two, or those of two from those of three years, and so on to the largest. No general rule as to their growth could be laid down, unless all the fish of one year had been hatched out at the same time, and enjoyed the same advantages of feed and range of water, up to the time of being caught. Still, in a brisk stream, I have generally considered a Trout of seven inches as being in its second summer; one of nine or ten in its third summer; a fish of twelve or thirteen in its fourth; and so on.

The Trout found in the deep still waters of the state of New York, though a variety of this species, are a third, or one-half larger at the same age, than the fish of our clear rapid streams; and as the rivers and lakelets there are less fished than the tributaries of the Delaware, Hudson, and Susquehanna, the Trout have a chance of growing older, and consequently larger. From my own observation, the average size of the adult fish in northern New York is at least double that of the fish taken in the streams flowing unto the rivers named above.

Some years ago, I had an afternoon's fishing in Hamilton County, when the catch was forty-five pounds. The fish averaged fourteen inches in length, and not less than a pound in weight. A friend on whose word I can rely, tells me he has taken three Trout of two pounds each, at a single cast, in the Raquette River, and repeated it several times in succession; and that he took off his drop-flies, to prevent a surfeit of sport, or too much strain on his light rod.

I have achieved something in the way of taking large Trout in Hamilton County, but after a man has satisfied the *sentiment* of camping out, and been bitten to his heart's content by mosquitoes and punkies, he prefers sleeping on a good straw bed, and enjoying the comforts of civilization, where although the fish are smaller, the streams are livelier and clearer, and it requires finer tackle and greater skill to take them.

There is a specific difference between our Brook Trout and the Common Trout *(Salmo fario)* of Great Britain. The Brook Trout when taken in its natural habitat (the clear rapid mountain stream), is a more symmetrical fish; its spot more brilliant; its sides of a brighter silvery hue; its flesh of finer flavor, though of lighter color; and its average size much smaller. The Trout of Hamilton and Franklin Counties, New York, are, as a general rule, not inferior in size to the Trout of England; their average is larger than those of the ponds of Long Island, and about equal to those taken *below* the ponds, where the fish have access to salt water.

I cannot agree with Frank Forester, that the Trout of Long Island are superior to those of our inland brooks and rivers; on the contrary, I think the pond Trout of Long Island much inferior in delicacy and flavor, though I admit, that those which have the run of both fresh and salt water are at least equal to those taken in mountain streams.

Fish inhabiting still, sluggish waters, dams, and lakelets, are of stouter proportions than those of rapid, tumbling streams. The difference is remarked by anglers who have fished the waters of Hamilton County; those of the lakes being deep of body and proportionately short, while those taken in the outlets

## Brook Trout. Speckled Trout.

are longer, and afford more sport when hooked. In some of the ponds of Long Island they are extremely stout; a Trout of twelve inches weighing a pound, which is four ounces more than one of the same length taken in a mountain stream would weigh.

I would here say, from personal knowledge of the fish, that the "Silver Trout" mentioned by Frank Forester as being taken in Green's Creek, on Long Island, is in every respect the same as those of the neighboring ponds. The lighter and more pearly hue is to be attributed entirely to the bright open creek flowing through a meadow, unshaded by trees, and communicating directly with the salt water of the bay.

All observing anglers have noticed the effect of water and light on the color of Trout; those taken in streams discolored from having their fountains in swamps, or flowing through boggy grounds where hemlock and juniper trees grow, are invariably dark, their spots less brilliant, and their sides and bellies frequently blurred; while those of bright streams flowing through open meadows or cultivated fields, are as remarkable for the deep vermilion of their spots, their light color, and delicate shading. Anglers who have fished the Tobyhanna and Broadhead's Creek, in Pennsylvania, will remember the color of the fish of these two streams; the former is boggy, much shaded, and the water almost the color of brandy; while the latter is clear, open, bright, and rapid. The Trout of the former are almost black, while those of the latter are light of color, and brilliant. I have seen anglers who could identify the Trout belonging to the different streams in the vicinity, when one turned out his catch from the creel.

Mr. Brown, in his "American Angler's Guide," says: "The Silver Trout or Common Trout is found in almost all of our clear, swift-running northern streams, and weighs from one to fifteen pounds. A splendid specimen of this species of Trout is found in Bashe's Kill, Sullivan County, New York." Mr. Brown was imposed on by the person on whose authority he makes this statement, for they are seldom if ever taken in Sullivan County above the weight of four pounds. Nor does an average catch in that or the adjoining counties exceed four or five ounces; nor is there any species called the "Silver Trout." The Black Trout also, which he describes as "found in muddy, sluggish streams with clay bottoms, in the roughest and wildest part of our country," is also nothing more nor less than our ordinary Brook Trout *(Salmo fontinalis)*, which, as already stated, becomes dark from inhabiting water discolored by vegetable infusion.

## Brook Trout. Speckled Trout.

Frank Forester's strictures on this disposition to claim a difference of species, on account of local or accidental causes producing a difference in size, condition, or color, are entirely appropriate, and he had good reasons for saying that the "Sea Trout" claimed by Mr. Smith of Massachusetts as a new species, was none other than a well-fed Brook Trout that had access to salt water, where its greater variety and abundance of food produced a brighter hue and deeper-colored flesh.

Mr. Brown, after quoting Mr. Smith's observations on the fish just referred to, says: "The last-mentioned species, *Lepomis salmonea*, is common in our Southern rivers, and with many Southerners goes under the name of Trout Bass, or Brown Bass." Mr. Brown here takes an error of Mr. Smith as a basis, and piles an error of his own, or that of his informer, on top of it, making "confusion worse confounded." Let me assure the reader that the so-called "Southern Trout" is not a Trout, nor has it the least generic affinity to it; it is a fresh-water Bass, *Grystes salmoides*, and belongs to the Perch family; and let me further say that there are no Trout, or any species of the Salmon family, found south of Virginia.

## FOOD OF TROUT

Flies, beetles, bugs, caterpillars, grasshoppers, in fact all manner of insects that are so unlucky as to touch the surface of the water, are arrested by the vigilant Trout; and little stonefish, minnows, and shiners are chased and devoured by them at night, in shoal water. I once opened a Trout of eleven inches, which appeared rather stout, and took from its pouch eight small shiners, which equalled nearly a fourth of its own weight. At another time, in a dark, still water, I took a Trout of twelve inches, which had nearly swallowed a water-lizard of six inches, the head of the victim protruding from the mouth of the fish; choked as he was with the lizard, he seized my fly. The little worm hatched from the egg of the fly (which a few days before, as she dapped on the surface of the water, she deposited at the risk of her life), is devoured with its little house of sand, in which, by the aid of its gluten, it encases itself. Hence the quantity of sand found in a Trout's stomach, in the early months of fly-fishing. The grasshopper is a good big mouthful; and sometimes as the angler grasps his prize, to disengage the hook, he feels them crush like rumpled paper, as if wings and legs were cracking beneath his fingers.

In watching the glassy surface of pools in the still of the evening, we see Trout dimpling the water with diverging circles, as they rise and suck in the little midge, or gray gnat, too small to be seen in the distance by the human eye. In every still water, or eddy, or hurrying rift, or under the shelving edges of stones, he searches for larva, diligent in earning his living "by the small;" or from his lair under ledge of rock or overhanging bank, he watches for larger prey as it floats past, seizing it with unerring and lightning-like rapidity.

Concerning the disposition of Trout to rise at a fly after having previously escaped from the angler with a hook fastened in its mouth, I would say that some years ago I took a Trout of ten inches out of a tumbling little hole under some alder-bushes, and to my surprise found what I thought to be a bristle sticking out of its mouth. On pulling hard on it, I drew the stomach of the fish up into its throat, and found the supposed bristle to be a stout piece of silkworm gut, four or five inches long, and a pretty ginger hackle on the end of it. I disengaged it, and on showing it to my fishing companion, he recognised it as his own drop-fly which a fish had broken from his leader, in the hole I described to him, three or four days before. He supposed the fish to have been at least twelve inches in length, when he lost his dropper. Only last summer a young fly-fisher of my acquaintance caught a Trout with a hook in his mouth, to which was fastened a gut-leader two feet long, and three good-sized shot on it, and yet the fish rose greedily at his red hackle. On returning to the house and showing the leader, it was claimed by a bait-fisherman, who had lost it the day before.

Brook Trout were once abundant in all the clear, rapid streams on the eastern side of the Alleghanies, from the Arctic regions to the thirty-eighth parallel, and even below it in the mountains of Virginia; in the upper tributaries of the Ohio, as well as in many of the northern streams flowing into the Mississippi; also in the smaller rivers which flow into the great chain of lakes from the north, and in many of those coming in from the south. They are taken frequently along the shores of Lake Superior, and in the more southern lakes, where creeks and brooks of a lower temperature than the lake itself fall in, and in the rapids at the great outlet of Lake Superior, known as Sault Ste. Marie. Most of the beautiful lakelets of New York, Maine, New Hampshire, and the Canadas, abound in Brook Trout of large size.

They are found also in many of the streams that flow eastward and southward from the Rocky Mountains; in the great basin between the latter range of mountains and the Sierra Nevada; and are numerous

## Brook Trout. Speckled Trout.

in the waters of the whole Pacific coast, as far down as the Bay of San Francisco, though perhaps with some distinction in variety, and, it may be, in species also.

In the rivers and brooks of the more settled part of the country, Trout have decreased both in numbers and size. This is to be attributed to many causes; to the clearing up of forests, exposing the surface of the ground to the sun, which has dried up the sources of sylvan brooks, or increased their temperature, and consequently that of the larger waters which they feed, rendering them less suitable for Trout, and promoting the introduction and increase of coarser families of fish. Streams which once had few fish besides Trout in them, now abound with Chub and other inferior fish. The saw-mill, with its high dam obstructing the passage of fish, and its saw-dust filling the pools below; the tannery, with its leached bark, and the discharge of lime mixed with impure animal matter extracted from the hides, flowing in and poisoning the Trout, have done more to depopulate our waters in a few years, than whole generations of anglers. It is an old story everywhere along our mountain streams, of how abundant Trout *once were;* and the angler is shocked and disgusted on every visit, with the unfair modes practised by the natives and pot-fishers in exterminating them.

## Norris on Trout Fishing

Trout were probably more abundant in our mountain streams at the time of the early settlement of the timber regions by the whites, than they were during the time of occupation by the Indians; for the red man, although he took no more than he could consume at the time, was a destructive fisher; his weirs and traps at the time of their autumnal descent, the spear on the spawning beds, and his snare or loop, were murderous implements; the proximity to good fishing-grounds was always a desideratum in placing his wigwam.

The rivers flowing into Lake Superior, as well as the outlet of that water, the Sault Ste. Marie, contain Brook Trout of large size. A friend who was on a north-west tour, during the summer of 1860, brought me the profile of a Trout, cut out of brown paper, with the following memoranda on it:—"Taken by J. E. Cady, of Sault Ste. Marie, July 30th 1858. Weight six and a quarter pounds, length twenty-four inches, circumference thirteen inches; at the same time took seven Trout from the same pool weighing thirty-one and a quarter pounds; taken in Batchewaunaung River, Canada West." This may appear improbable, but the gentleman who presented it, and the captor, are both truthful men.

*Brook Trout. Speckled Trout.*

I have lately been shown a letter which stated that a party of three anglers went last summer from Chicago by rail and boat, to the town of Green Bay, and there packed their luggage on mules and travelled a distance of forty miles to a stream not over twenty feet wide, within twelve miles of Lake Superior. They fished two pools where there was neither tree nor bush to interfere with their fly-cast, and during their stay of ten days, each of them killed from fifty to a hundred pounds of Trout per day; the fish weighing from two to four pounds each. In the state of Maine, Lake Umbagog and Moosehead Lake have great reputation. The tributaries of the St. John and Mirimichi have many and large Trout; and from all accounts they fairly swarm in Lake Nipissiguit, at the head of the river of that name, in the British Province of New Brunswick.

*Head of a large brook trout*

Mr. B., an angler of this city, a few years ago, brought home from Maine, where he had been on a fishing excursion, the skin of a Trout, which he has since had stuffed; the weight of the fish exceeded eight pounds.

The following was clipped from the "Saturday Evening Post" last summer, and handed to me by a friend:—

"ENORMOUS TROUT.—Mr. George S. Page, of the firm of George S. Page & Brother, of this city, has shown us a basket of Trout, caught—he says it does not matter where, and he would rather not disclose the precise locality—but which are by far the largest of their kind we have ever seen. In the basket before us the heaviest fish weighs eight pounds and three-eighths; another weighs eight pounds and a quarter; and another, seven and a quarter pounds. Two others weighed six pounds and a quarter and six pounds; one weighed five and a half, and two five pounds each.

"These fish are all the catch of two gentlemen, Mr. Page and Mr. R. O. Stanley, of Maine, in the early part of the present month. In eight days they caught two hundred and seventy-three pounds, steelyard weight, and the fish caught averaged three and a half pounds each.

## Brook Trout. Speckled Trout.

"Mr. Page desires us to say that all these fish were caught in fair play, with the fly. Trout-fishermen must look out for their laurels."

If these fish were caught in the St. Croix River or its tributaries in Maine, they may have been the Schoodic Trout, *Salmo Gloveri*. One who is not accustomed to mark specific differences, may easily have been deceived, though there are some instances of Brook Trout exceeding even the size of the Schoodic Trout.

Sir Humphrey Davy, in his "Salmonia," gives the reader the impression that in strictly preserved streams in England, Trout under two pounds are not basketed, but returned to the water. This is by no means a general rule. Last summer, in looking over an English angler's fly-book with him, he produced his written authority, signed by the steward of some nobleman, I think the Duke of Northumberland, to fish a certain water. The paper specified that the catch of the angler should at any time be subject to the inspection of the gamekeeper and that he should basket no fish under *four inches*.

# CHAPTER THREE

# *Trout Fly-Fishing.— The Stream.*

*Casting the Fly.—Theory of strict imitation.—Striking and killing a Fish.—Likely places, how to fish them.*

## CASTING THE FLY

So much has been written on this subject, that the learner who consults the *authorities,* not only finds that "doctors disagree," but that he is bewildered with what may appear to him unnecessary detail; and he is thus impressed with an idea that Fly-Fishing is a science to be attained only with much study and practice. It would therefore be much better to learn the rudiments from some skilful friend on the stream, and afterwards read such authorities as Chitty, "Ephemera," and Ronalds.

As it is likely, however, that some of my readers who may wish to try their hands, may not be able to avail themselves of the practical instruction of friends

*Trout Fly-Fishing.—The Stream.*

of experience, or may not have access to English authors on fly-fishing, I will, with some misgivings as to my ability to profit them, describe the usual manner of casting the fly, as practised by our best anglers. Advising the beginner not to be ambitious at first of accomplishing what he may deem a difficult feat, that is, to cast a long line, but rather by patience and diligence to acquire the knack of delivering one of moderate length straight out and lightly; by perseverance he will in due time find "how use doth breed a habit in a man."

On a favorable day the learner, with faith and industry, and no preconceived notions of the difficulty of fly-fishing, may find at his nooning that he has made a catch which does not compare unfavorably with that of his more skilful brother. If the contrary be the case, let him not lose heart, as there may have been many circumstances against him; as inexperience of the waters, the arrangement of his whip, landing his fish, &c., which he has yet to learn, and that it is not his casting which is altogether at fault.

Some writers have objected to the accepted term "whipping," contending that casting the fly is different from whipping with a long staff and lash. I acknowledge that in the main it is. Still the first motions of the arm and rod are not unlike the motions of the arm and whip-staff of a stage-driver. The latter intends that the end of his lash shall reach a certain part of the horse's body, while the angler intends that his flies shall fall on a certain part of the stream; but here the similitude ends. The driver, by a sudden backward motion of the arm, causes the lash to strike the horse with force, and rebound; while the angler avoids the quick backward motion, and allows his flies to fall lightly; and then, not hastily, but by a gentle movement of his rod, draws his flies towards him or across the water.

But to commence.—Let the beginner draw out as much line as he can conveniently cast. If he uses a twelve foot rod, eighteen feet (that is, from the tip to the stretcher-fly) is enough. Then with a backward motion of his rod, let his line go well out behind him, and before it has time to fall to the ground, by a forward motion of the forearm and wrist, cast his flies to the desired place on the water.

The *backward* motion of the line is chiefly imparted by the spring of the rod, as the flies are lifted from the water, and if it does not go to its full length behind, it will come down clumsily on the water before the angler, when he casts it forward, and short of the place aimed at. The same bad effect is produced by using too much force. The beginner should bear in mind that it is not strength, but an easy sleight, and the spring of the rod, that effects the long and light cast. The arm should be extended slightly, and the motion imparted to the rod by the forearm working as on a pivot at the elbow, and the hand turning as on another pivot at the wrist. The motion of the hand and wrist only is required in a short, straight cast.

The angler should not cast at random over the water, but each portion of it should be carefully fished, the nearest first. He should always aim at some particular place; he will soon learn to measure the distance with his eye, and exert the exact amount of force to propel his flies to the desired spot. In drawing them over the water, the primary object is to have the drop-fly to skim or dap along on the surface; the stretcher which follows in its wake may be allowed to take care of itself, for, as a general thing, it matters little whether it is on or beneath the surface.

When the flies first fall on the water, they should be allowed to rest a moment, and the slight motion imparted by tightening the line, or in recovering the full grasp of the rod on the instant, should be avoided. If in the current, they should be left for some moments to its will, then guided gently and

## Trout Fly-Fishing.—The Stream.

sometimes with a tremulous motion across or diagonally up against it.

After the learner (and he will always be learning) has acquired the first principles of the art, necessity, ingenuity, and observation will teach him how to cast in difficult places. Our streams and lakes are generally fished, the first by wading, the latter from a boat, and seldom from a high bank. It is therefore less necessary to cast a long line than many suppose, or English writers describe it to be. But our rugged forest streams, overhung by bushes and branches of trees, and other obstructions occurring, make it requisite that the angler should acquire tact and skill, to meet these difficulties.

In casting under branches which hang within a few feet of the water, the motion of the rod and course pursued by the line is necessarily horizontal. For instance, in wading down a stream, if you intend whipping under the branches on the right, a backhanded cast is necessary; the backward preparatory motion of the rod being across the stream to your left, and the cast horizontally from the left to your right. When the branches you wish to cast under are on your left, the course of the line is vice versa, that is, from the right to the left.

The largest Trout love the shade of trees and bushes which overhang the bank, and it is only by the means just described that you can present your flies. It is customary to fish down stream, and there is much difference of opinion as to whether the general rule should be to cast directly down or across the water. In this the angler must be governed much by circumstances, and his own judgment. I prefer the diagonal cast, as presenting the flies in a more natural way, although the drop-fly may appear to play better, and set more at right angles with the leader, when drawing up against the stream.

When the wind is blowing up the stream, it becomes in a good degree necessary to fish across, if possible casting below the desired spot, and allowing the wind to carry the flies to the right place as they fall on the water. If, however, it blows strongly in the direction of the cast, care should be taken when putting on a fresh fly to moisten the gut to which it is attached, if it be a stretcher. Many flies are cracked off by neglecting this precaution.

The advice of English writers to fish *up stream,* or with the wind at one's back, in most cases cannot be followed; for our rough rapid streams in the first instance, and the thickly-wooded banks in the other, which make it necessary to wade, ignore both rules.

## Trout Fly-Fishing.—The Stream.

The force of the current in many a good rift would bring the flies back, and, as I have seen with beginners, entangle them in the legs of his pantaloons. It is only in a still pool, or where the current is gentle, that one is able to fish up stream with any degree of precision.

A word or two here about the flies coming down

"Light as falls the flaky snow,"

and that the flies *only* should touch the surface, or that they should touch it before the leader. The first idea is a very poetical one, and may be carried out in a good degree, if the line is light, the leader fine, and the cast not too long. The second is impracticable with a long line, unless from a bank somewhat elevated above the water. But in a day's fishing on our streams, the miraculous casting or falling of the flies, which some writers speak of, and their skill in this respect, are things we "read about."

My experience is, that the falling of the leader—which is almost transparent when properly dyed—does not frighten the fish, but it is the incautious approach or conspicuous position of the angler. In casting over a piece of water, the flies always precede the leader and line, and, as a matter of course, fall where the fish lie before the line does, as the fisher advances or extends his cast. As the line *will* swag more or less in a long cast, it must necessarily touch the water.

I would not give the impression from the foregoing that it is not necessary that the flies should fall lightly, for in fishing fine it is important that they should. To accomplish this, as I have already said, no sudden check should be given to the flies, but they should be eased off (if I may so express it) as they fall, by the slightest downward bending of the wrist.

There is a great deal of poetry also, as well as fiction, in the stories told about casting a very long line. Experience will teach you to cast no longer line than is necessary, whatever proficiency you may acquire. Still it should be borne in mind, that the higher your position above the water, the more visible you are to the fish, hence the greater the necessity for fishing far off when occupying such a stand. But with such elevation, it is easier to cast a long line. When a person is wading the stream, he is less visible to the fish than if he was on the bank, as the medium through which the line of sight passes is more dense than the atmosphere above, and the rougher the water the more the line of sight between the angler and the fish is disturbed.

## Trout Fly-Fishing.—The Stream.

Nicer casting is, of course, required on a still pool than on a rift; a careful angler, when he wades such water, will always go in softly, without floundering or splashing, fishing it by inches, scarcely making a ripple, and creating so slight a disturbance, that he will find the fish rising within a few yards of him; then he should cast with not too long a line, and lightly. If he sees a large Trout rising lower down the pool, he does not fish carelessly, or hurry on to get to him, but tries to take those that may lie in the intervening water, and approaches him slowly and imperceptibly, knowing that he will be found there when his time comes. I may add here that in such water a landing-net is indispensable, as it would disturb the pool to wade ashore with every good fish, and that here also you have a better opportunity of using your net and securing your fish, than in a rift.

In casting a long line, or even a short one, particularly on a windy day, it is better to wet it occasionally by holding the leader and flies in your hand, and let it swag in the water; the weight of the line thus increased, helps the cast. If it could be accomplished, the great desideratum would be, to keep the line wet and the flies dry. I have seen anglers succeed so well in their efforts to do this by the means just mentioned, and by whipping the moisture from their flies, that the stretcher and dropper would fall so lightly, and remain so long on the surface, that a fish would rise and deliberately take the fly before it sank.

One instance of this kind is fresh in my memory: it occurred at a pool beneath the fall of a dam on the Williwemock, at a low stage of water—none running over. The fish were shy and refused every fly I offered them, when my friend put on a Grannom for a stretcher, and a minute Jenny Spinner for a dropper. His leader was of the finest gut and his flies fresh, and by cracking the moisture from them between each throw, he would lay them so lightly on the glassy surface, that a brace of Trout would take them at almost every cast, and before they sank or were drawn away. He had tied these flies and made his whip especially for his evening cast on this pool, and as the fish would not notice mine, I was obliged to content myself with landing his fish, which in a half hour counted several dozen. Here was an exemplification of the advantage of keeping one's flies dry, and the fallacy of the theory of not allowing the line to fall on the water, for in this instance I noticed that a fourth or a third of it touched the surface at every cast.

It seems to me that there is no more appropriate place than this to say a few words about the "routine" and "strict imitation system," which some English

## TROUT FLIES

GROUSE HACKLE

GINGER HACKLE

YELLOW SALLY

ALDER FLY

RED SPINNER

DOTTEREL

A PALMER

COACHMAN

GRAY DRAKE—
A MAY FLY

*Norris's basic selection of wet flies was mostly derived or adapted from older British patterns. Note the great variety of body shapes and lengths, hackling styles, and wing styles. As Norris's own opinions suggest, American anglers were already debating various theories of imitation and experimenting with new fly patterns.*

writers advocate so strenuously. The former, that is, certain flies for certain months, or for each month, is now considered an exploded theory by practical anglers who wish to divest fly-fishing of all pedantic humbug; for the fly that is good in April is killing in August, and the Red and Brown Hackle, the Coachman, Alder-Fly, and Brown Hen, will kill all summer.

For the theory of "strict imitation," there is some show of reason, but I cannot concede that Trout will rise more readily at the artificial fly which most closely resembles the natural one, for the fish's attention is first attracted because of something lifelike falling on the water, or passing over the surface, and he rises at it because he supposes it to be something he is in the habit of feeding upon, or because it resembles an insect or looks like a fly, not that it is any *particular* insect or fly; for we sometimes see the most glaring cheat, which resembles nothing above the waters or beneath the waters, a piece of red flannel, for instance, or the fin of one of their own species, taken greedily.

The last time I had positive proof of this was some years ago, when I happened to spend a quiet Sabbath in the "Beech Woods" of Pennsylvania, with a cheery Irishman who had made a clearing on the

Big Equinunk. Towards noon I missed my creel, and on inquiring what had become of it, was told that the boys had gone a-fishing and taken it with them. In the afternoon they returned with the creel full of Trout, which far exceeded my catch of the day previous. I asked them if they had taken them with worms—no; with the fly—no, they had none; and then I remembered the "dodge" I had practised myself in my early Trout-fishing days. They said they had "skittered" with the *belly fin* of the Trout. A worm to catch the first fish was the only bait they wanted, all the rest of the Trout were taken by drawing this rude counterfeit over the surface of the water. They did not know—happy little fellows—that their practice was in opposition to the theory of learned professors,—Hofland, Blaine, Shipley, Ronalds, and others.

## STRIKING AND KILLING A FISH

*Striking.*—Various directions have been given about striking a fish when it rises at the fly. Some maintain that it is unnecessary, or even wrong, to strike at all, if the line is kept taut. Others say that you should strike as soon as you see the fish or the swirl he makes as he turns to go back. Either is wrong, if adopted as a rule without exceptions.

In most cases when Trout rise freely, and are in earnest, they will hook themselves, for the yielding of a pliant rod, as a fish takes the fly, allows him to bear off his prize; but when he attempts to cast it from his mouth, the spring of the rod fixes the hook in his mouth, as he relaxes his hold. So it frequently happens that the rise is seen and the strain on the rod is felt at the same moment. A fish may even miss the fly, and make another effort to seize it, if not drawn away too hastily. When a fish, therefore, takes the fly vigorously, it is only necessary to keep the line taut. A mere turn of the wrist may be given to fix the hook more firmly in his mouth.

On the contrary, when the water is subsiding after a freshet, and the fish have been feeding on worms and insects which have been washed in, they will frequently tug at your stretcher, taking it for such food. Then it is necessary to strike sharply. I have sometimes fished all day in this way, allowing the stretcher (generally a red hackle) to sink a little, and trolling as with a bait, and striking when I felt a bite. Again, on warm days, when Trout lie beneath the shade of trees which stretch their branches over deep still pools, they will rise almost without ruffling the surface, or softly arrest the stretcher beneath, as if to ascertain if it is really something to eat; then a slight

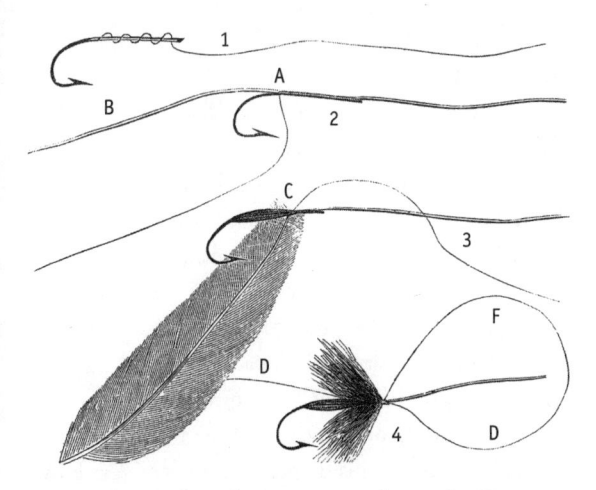

*Norris's instructions for tying a simple wet fly. Note that a gut "snell" was tied to the hook first; in the 1860s, almost all trout flies were tied on eyeless hooks.*

but quick stroke is necessary to secure the fish before he casts it from his mouth.

*Killing a Fish.*—Many Trout are lost by the beginner, from excitement or a lack of judgment in managing them. It is always the safer plan to handle a fish as if he was slightly hooked, and in fishing a rift, to get him out of the rough water and towards the margin where it is comparatively still, as soon as possible. For in his efforts to escape, you have the force of the current, as well as his strength and agility, to contend with.

If the water is still, and the fish indisposed to show fight, tow him gently to one side and then to the other, as you reel in the line. If there is a sloping shore without obstructions, and you think he is securely hooked, you may sometimes get a little headway on him, and, by a steady pull, lead him ashore before he overcomes his astonishment at being hooked, or has realized his danger. If in landing a fish in this way, though, you allow him to come in contact with a stone or other impediment, it will arouse all his fears, and in his desperation he may tear loose.

When a fish of unusual size is hooked, and you can do so without disturbing the lower end of the rift or pool, it is safer to lead him down stream, for this increases the difficulty of his breathing, while you are assisted by the current, and the strain on your tackle is diminished.

English writers direct us, after hooking a fish, to keep the rod in a perpendicular position, or the point well back over the shoulder; this is very well if he is securely hooked and swims deep. If he struggles and flounders on the surface, though, the point should be immediately lowered, and the rod held nearly horizontally across the stream, giving him the whole spring of it, thus keeping him under. It is better not to raise his head above the water until he is somewhat exhausted, or until you are ready to slip the landing-net under him.

If your reel has a moderately stiff click, and the fish is large enough to run the line off, he should be allowed to do so, bearing on him with the line unchecked by the slightest pressure of the fingers. As he slacks in his resistance, reel in the line, giving when you must and shortening when you can, "butting him," as some persons call it, or bearing hard, only when he approaches some dangerous place, and leading him away from it. After you have ventured to raise his head above water, give to any strong effort he may make to get beneath, or to his humor to take another run, but bearing on him all the while with a taut line. When you can venture to bring him near, reel in until the end of the leader, where it joins the line, has reached the end of the tip; he is then, if the leader is three-fourths the length of the rod, and the rod pliant, close enough to slip your net under him. This should be done not with a swoop, but gently; seize him with the left hand, sticking your thumb under his gill, and taking the hook out of his mouth put him tail-foremost into the hole of your creel.

*Norris did not illustrate a trout reel in detail, but his salmon reel, probably of brass, was typical of the simple, sturdy designs of the day.*

There is much less strain on one's tackle in playing a fish than is generally supposed. In killing a Salmon, if he is properly handled, it does not exceed a pound, and with a Trout, it is not over an ounce or two.

I have known anglers handle fish so well as to make a common practice of slipping the hand gently down the leader, and seizing them behind the gills, sometimes wearing a thread glove to insure a firmer grasp. Few, however, have sufficient skill and coolness for such dangerous practice. A landing-net is almost indispensable when there is no convenient place for leading your prize to the bank, or when wading ashore would disturb the quiet of a pool.

## LIKELY PLACES, AND HOW TO FISH THEM

The success of the fly-fisher depends almost as much on what might be called an intuitive knowledge of likely places, as his skill in casting, or in killing a fish.

The beginner generally prefers a lively rift, where there is an open cast, for the current takes a good hold on his stretcher, and bears it down stream, while it keeps his leader taut, and his dropper dapping prettily on the surface. But he should remember that in most cases, at such a cast, he is likely to be exposed to the view of the fish, which always lie with their heads up stream. He should therefore approach cautiously, fishing the slack water on each side at the head of the rift, with as long a line as he can well manage. Coming nearer step by step and casting as he advances, he will fish the near, and then the opposite side lower down, drawing his flies lightly across the rough water, and submitting them in some degree to its will. Still approaching he will cast obliquely across, then straight down and over the water where the current abates.

As a general rule the larger fish take precedence, and lie nearer the head of a rift and rise first. If found at the lower end, it will be where the water is deeper and where there are rocks or an overhanging bank. Trout are not often found in a rift or pool with a smooth even floor of rock, or small pebbles, as it affords them no harbor or hiding-places.

Where a large rock projects above the surface in water of sufficient depth, the angler should cast near its edges on both sides, then above where it repels the force of the stream; or he may have a rise in the eddy just below, where the divided current unites again.

A deep bend in the stream where a caving bank overhangs, affords a likely cast, especially where stumps, logs, or drift-wood lie about.

If the stream has a long still reach, one generally fishes from the shallower side, finding his cast opposite where it is deeper, casting close to, or under the pendent boughs, or in the shade of the bushes or trees—drawing his flies diagonally or directly across. It is not a bad plan when fish have risen and refused one's flies, in such a pool, to sit patiently down and change them for smaller ones of different colors, and after a little while "try back," that is, fish from the lower to the upper end. Different flies cast from another direction will sometimes induce fish to "reconsider the motion," and adopt your amendment if properly presented.

*Trout Fly-Fishing.—The Stream.*

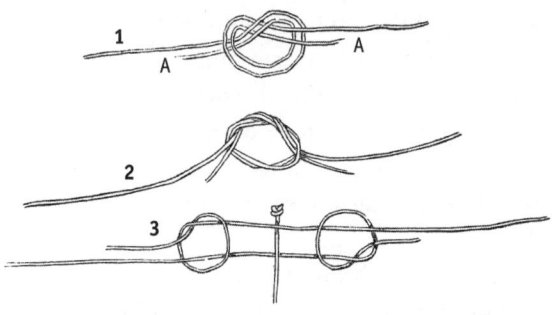

*Norris recommended three knots for the purposes of fly fishers. Number 1, the "angler's single knot," was used for simply connecting sections of line. Number 2, the "angler's double knot," was preferred for attaching sections of silkworm gut together more securely. Number 3, the "water knot," enabled the fly fisher to connect a dropper's snell with the knot that joined two sections of silkworm gut. The dropper's snell is the downward-extending line with the small knot on its upper end.*

When the season is well advanced—say July or August, Trout will assemble in pairs or little communities in some suitable place for spawning, and remain there if there is no excessive rise in the stream, until it is time to spawn. This is frequently beneath the overhanging alders; there *chuck* your flies under, if you cannot present them more civilly, and if you take a good fish, try again, for the rest are likely to be as hungry. If the sun be bright, use the Alder-fly on such occasions, for either dropper or stretcher, or both. The same kind of a shallow side-rift is a likely place early in June when the Suckers congregate there to spawn, and the Trout are on the lookout a few yards below, to catch their roe as it is carried down stream by the current.

Immediately below a mill-dam, if there be any depth of water, is invariably a good place; but you should never stand conspicuously above on what is called "the breast" of the dam, or on a high rock; such a position is to be condemned even in a bait-fisher; but get below, and if there is no way of fishing from the sides, go to the tail of the pool, and cast upwards. This, if there be but little water coming over the dam, is the best place to fish from. Trout will not take the fly immediately under the fall or in the foam, but a little below.

In a deep still pool much exposed to the sun, if there is a tree or two on the bank with drooping boughs, Trout are apt to collect there, for they love the shade. Here, if the weather is warm, they are not apt to rise with a splash, as I have just remarked, but will suck in your fly with a mere dimpling of the water, or you may have a vague sense of its being arrested beneath the surface. Then strike sharply, but do not be violent, and you have him; try again, there are more there; and good ones.

Never pass a piece of still water of reasonable depth where a fresh spring brook, however diminutive, comes in, particularly in warm weather. I have in my memory such a pool bordered on one side with hair-grass and duck-weed, which I had frequently passed heedlessly by, supposing it to be backwater from the main stream, or left in the old bed of the creek, from the overflow of the spring freshets. But one day, seeing a quiet dimpling of the surface, I waded lazily in, and threw my flies carelessly on the water, when a thirteen-incher laid hold, and was away in the duck-weed before I recovered from my astonishment. After many turns, however, and much contention, the pliant little rod exhausted him. Thus encouraged, I fished the shaded pool its whole length as noiselessly as an otter, and the result was a dozen very handsome Trout. I never passed that pool again without giving it the attention it merited.

Sometimes on the subsiding of a freshet, Trout will surmount a long rapid, and rest in a pool, or the smooth flow of water above, where it is not a half yard in depth. Fish such water with as long a cast as possible, and so as not to throw your shadow over the swim.

A brisk clattering little brook, as it rushes along over rocks and logs, through the woods, washes out many a pretty hole in its sharp turns, and amongst the big stones, where the laurel and alders render casting impossible. The only way here is, let the current carry your flies down stream, until the dropper bobs enticingly on the water. Play them on each side of the little rift, drawing them towards you and allowing them to drift off again. If there are fish in the hole they will be jumping at the dropper, or tugging at the stretcher. Three to one they will hook themselves; if they don't, strike gently at each tug or jump, as if you were fishing with a bait, but not drawing your flies entirely from the water. I have taken good fish in the small tributaries of a larger stream in this way, the monarch of the rift always first, and his successors in order, according to size. The head of a mill-dam, where a rapid meets the back-water, is invariably a good place.

I have already said or intimated, that on a bright day Trout will always rise better in the shade. Therefore when a pool is of equal depth across, one side of it may be better in the morning, and the other side in the afternoon. There are many good pools also which are not shaded on either side, or where persons pass frequently, or show themselves to the fish;

here they scarcely rise until after sundown. Such places are often fished without success by an angler, and in a very short time one who follows him may have good sport. The largest fish are nearly always taken after the sun is down, or at least off the water.

But of all places commend me in the still of the evening, to the long placid pool, shallow on one side, with deeper water and an abrupt overhanging bank opposite. Where the sun has shone all day, and legions of ephemera sported in its declining rays; the bloom of the rye or clover scent-

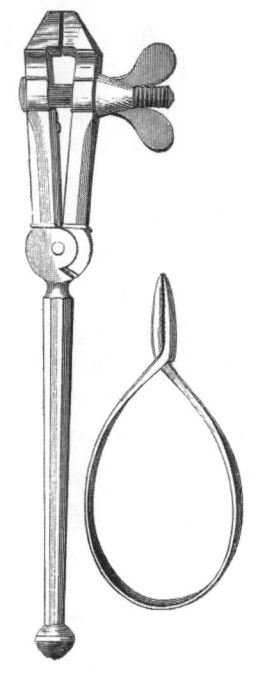

*Norris's fly-tying vise and hackle pliers, universally common implements for fly tiers then and now.*

ing the air from the adjoining field! Now light a fresh pipe, and put on a pale Ginger Hackle for your tail-fly, and a little white-winged Coachman for your dropper. Then wade in cautiously—move like a shadow—don't make a ripple. Cast, slowly, long, light; let your stretcher sink a little. There he has taken the Ginger—lead him around gently to the shallow side as you reel him in, but don't move from your position—let him tug awhile, put your net under him, break his neck, and slip him into your creel. Draw your line through the rings—cast again; another, and another. Keep on until you can see only the ripple made by your fly; or know when it falls, by the slight tremor it imparts through the whole line down to your hand—until the whip-poor-will begins his evening song, and the little water-frog tweets in the grass close by.—Not till then is it time to go home.

If you have dined on the stream, it may be that the Trout you roasted were too highly seasoned and you are thirsty; if so, stop at the old spring by the roadside.

## CHAPTER FOUR

# *The Michigan Grayling.*

Until within a few years, that portion of Michigan extending from the forty-fourth parallel to the Straits of Mackinaw, dotted with beautiful lakes and traversed by many a clear, winding river, was *terra incognita* to the fly-fisher; and although we were told years ago by explorers and adventurous anglers that trout in great numbers and of large size were taken in the waters of the northern portion of the peninsula, the grayling by its true name was unknown, and does not now form a subject for any of our angling authors. It was supposed that, except in the Arctic regions, it did not exist on our continent. About ten years ago, however, hunters, and those who were looking up timber lands, began to talk of a white-meated fish with all the game qualities of the trout, which they captured in streams of both water-sheds—east and west—as an addition to their venison and "hard-tack." It was known to them as the "white trout," the "Crawford County trout," and under other local names, until a specimen in alcohol was sent to Professor E. D. Cope, of the Philadelphia Academy of Natural Sciences, who described it in the proceedings of that institution in the year 1865, and gave it the scientific name of *Thymallus tricolor,* the generic name arising from the fresh thyme-y smell of the fish when first taken from the water, the specific appellation having reference to its beautiful dorsal fin. And yet its discovery as a true grayling escaped the notice of nearly all of our fly-fishers; and to the few who might have meditated an expedition in search of it, its habitat was far off, and then almost inaccessible. The following passage, however, from "American Fish Culture" (p. 196), by the present writer, and published by Porter & Coates, in 1867, soon after Professor Cope described the fish, attracted the notice of Mr. J. V. Le Moyne, of Chicago.

"While on a trout-fishing excursion lately in the northern part of Pennsylvania, I met a very intelligent, though not a scientific person, who informed me that in exploring some timber lands on the Au Sable, in Michigan, he came across a new kind of trout which he had never seen before. From his

*The Michigan Grayling.*

*The Michigan Grayling*

description it was doubtless this new species of *Thymallus*. He said it readily took a bait of a piece of one of its fellows, a piece of meat being used to capture the first fish; and that it was very beautiful and of delicious flavor."

The following summer, after consulting persons interested in timber lands, Mr. Le Moyne packed his "kit" and found his way by steamer to Little Traverse Bay, and thence by canoe through a series of lakes to the River Jordan, where he had great sport, not only with grayling, but with trout of good size, taking both from the same pool, and not unfrequently one of each on the same cast. I may here mention that the Jordan is one of the few streams of Michigan in which both are found. Trout are unknown in the Manistee and Au Sable. My friend, Mr. D. H.

Fitzhugh, Jr., of Bay City, the year following, took them in the Rifle and went by a new railroad then being built to the Hersey and Muskegon, walking twenty miles of the distance. He had been waiting with much interest the extension of the Jackson, Lansing, and Saginaw Railroad northward, and in 1873, when it crossed the Au Sable, he launched his boat high up on that lovely river. Since then the fame of the rare sporting qualities of this fish has spread among anglers, and they now come from many of our large towns and cities (especially those of the West) to camp on the banks of the Michigan rivers and enjoy the sport.

The European species *(T. vexillifer)* is mentioned by all English authors on angling from the time of Dame Juliana Berners to the present. The opinion is advanced by some of them that it was introduced into England when under the religious sway of the see of Rome, as it is generally found in rivers near the ruins of old monasteries. Sir Humphrey Davy, in his "Salmonia" (1828), wrote of it as inhabiting the Avon, the Ure, the Nye, and the Dee; and Hofland (1839), in addition to those, mentions the Trent, the Dove, the Derwent, the Wharfe, and a few other rivers. Sir Humphrey Davy also tells us that it is found in some of the streams of the Alpine valleys, and, he intimates, in some of the rivers of Sweden and Norway. A friend of the writer, who of late years has been in the habit of spending his summers in Bavaria, has had fair sport with grayling in the Isar and Traun, near Munich and Traunstein, as also in the Inn and Salza, and mentions the names of a few quiet English anglers who come annually in September to fish these rivers.

European waters, however, were probably never as prolific of grayling as those of Michigan; for trout, which feed largely on the young of all fish, are there found in the same streams. In Michigan rivers where grayling most abound there are no trout, and the fry of their own and other species are never found in their stomachs. The various orders of flies which lay their eggs in running water, and the larvæ of such flies, appear to be their only food.

Writers in sporting papers have recently claimed that grayling have also been found in the older States of the Union. If this be the fact, they are now extinct. They are said to exist in some few of the rivers of Wisconsin, which is quite probable, and also in Montana and Dakota. Dr. Richardson, in his "Fauna Boreali-Americana," gives not only a glowing description of the exquisite beauty of Back's grayling *(T. signifer)*, but speaks with all the ardor of a true angler of its game qualities. The Esquimaux title, *Hewlook powak,* denoting wing-like fin, he says, alludes to its magnificent dorsal, which, as in the Michigan grayling, exceeds in size and beauty that of the European species.

Grayling, wherever found, are spring spawners, as also are the smelt and the capelin or spearling. All other genera of the salmon family spawn in autumn. The usual time with grayling, both here and in Europe, is the latter part of April and early in May. They do not push for the very sources of rivers, leaping falls and flapping sidewise over shallows to find some little rivulet as trout do, but deposit their ova in the parts of the stream where they are taken, or, if such portions are not of the proper temperature, they will sometimes seek the mouths of smaller and cooler affluents. The time of their spawning is limited to a few days or a week or so. Of the experts who have gone to the Au Sable to express the ova, fertilize it, and bring it East to introduce this fish into the Atlantic States, one found that they were not ready to spawn, and the next season, another, who went a week or so later, found that they had spawned. I have taken fry as long as my little finger on the first of September, which were the produce of eggs spawned in April. Those that came from ova of the preceding

## The Michigan Grayling.

year were six inches long; at two years old, they are ten or twelve inches long; at three years old, they are thirteen to fifteen inches long; and at four years, sixteen or seventeen inches, and weigh from three-quarters of a pound to a pound and a quarter; each succeeding year adding proportionately less to their length and more to their girth. An abundance or deficiency of food, however, has much influence on their growth, while some are naturally more thrifty than others. Sir Humphrey Davy says: "Grayling hatched in June become in the same year, in September or October, nine or ten inches long, and weigh from half a pound to ten ounces, and the next year are from twelve to fifteen inches." On this point, as will be seen from the foregoing, I differ with him, I think he must have written from hearsay.

In Michigan, in a day's fishing, the true-hearted angler returns to the water a great many more than he puts in his live-box. He will keep none under a half pound, and where the streams are so abundantly stocked, he will not begrudge their liberty to all under that weight. Our grayling are much more slender than the European species, but, if we credit English authors, do not attain as large a size. Three-fourths of a pound with us is a good average size, and one of a pound and a quarter is considered a large fish. I have *heard,* however, of their being taken in the Jordan over three pounds. The grayling is a fish of more symmetrical proportions than the trout, although it has not the vermilion spots and bright colors over its body, but its head and mouth are much smaller, and with handsome, prominent eyes. Its habits also differ materially from those of the trout. It is never found in the strong, turbulent water at the head of a rift, but in the deeper portions of the smoothly gliding stream. It avoids a bottom of clay or the mosses so common to the beds of Michigan rivers, but is always found on gravel or sand. Its rise is straight up—sharp and sudden, and when its attention is once drawn to the artificial line, it does not turn back, as a trout does, on getting a sight of the angler, but in its eagerness disregards him entirely, and in running a river with the speed of the current, or even if the boat is poled along down stream, it frequently takes the fly within a few feet of the pole or the boat. Its play is quite as vigorous as that of the trout, and it leaps frequently above the surface of the water before it is sufficiently exhausted to be drawn in. There is this difference, however, between the two. The trout, like a certain denomination of Christians, seems to believe in "final perseverance," and will kick and struggle to the last, even as it

## The Michigan Grayling.

is lifted in; while the grayling, after you have sufficiently overcome its obstinate pluck to get its head above water, is taken in with pendent tail, as much as to say, "It's all up"; but as soon as it touches the floor of the boat, its flapping and floundering begin. If it takes a sheer across the current, with its large dorsal fin, it offers greater resistance than the trout. Where they are so numerous, one seldom uses the landing-net, for few escape by breaking away, and if they do, there are more to take hold at the next cast.

If in fishing with a whip of three flies the angler hooks a fish on either of his droppers, the stretcher fly as it sails around beneath is pretty sure of enticing another, and not unfrequently the disengaged dropper hooks a third fish. Sometimes, as I have sat on the cover of the live-box, I have looked down to see three of these bright fish, after I had exhausted them, all in a row, their dorsal fins erect and waving in the clear water like so many beautiful leaves of the coleus. Nor is the grayling in taking a fly as chary a fish as the trout. On a perfectly still water you may see the latter rising and taking in the minute natural flies, when the veriest artificial midge will not tempt it; but let even a light breeze spring up and a ripple appear on the surface, and then it cannot distinguish the natural from the artificial, and will take hold. The grayling, on the contrary, is the most eager, unsophisticated fish imaginable. When it sees anything bearing the most remote semblance of life, it "goes for it," even if the water is as smooth as a mirror.

The whole of Michigan south of the Straits of Mackinaw may certainly be called flat country. The only rising grounds to be found are a few sandy eminences,—they can scarcely be called hills,—the formation of which we leave the geologist to account for. And yet the rivers abrading against these sandhills occasionally cause precipitous bluffs (few of which exceed a hundred feet), or such an elevation as is known in a lumberman's parlance as a "roll-way."

There is a gradual but almost imperceptible elevation from Bay City or Grand Rapids to the region where grayling are found. From the former to Grayling, where the railroad crosses the Au Sable, a distance of nearly a hundred miles, there is a rise of seven hundred feet, which gives the rivers an average current of about two and a half miles an hour. Wherever there is a contraction in the width of the stream, however, especially around a bend, its velocity may be three, four, or even five miles, but on account of the absence of rocks in the bottom, it almost invariably flows smoothly. The strength of the current can only be seen where the ends of half-sunken logs or

## The Michigan Grayling.

*Fishing Michigan's Manistee River in the 1870s was a wilderness adventure for the aging Norris.*

"sweepers" project above the surface, or when the canoeman turns his prow up-stream.

The grayling region on the Lake Huron watershed has a top stratum of coarse white sand. On the streams flowing toward Lake Michigan, the sand is yellow, with more or less admixture of vegetable loam. The rains falling on these sandy plains and percolating through meet with a lower stratum of impervious clay, and thus form under-ground courses which crop out at the margin or in the beds of the streams and keep them at the temperature of spring water.

The eighth longitudinal line west from Washington may be considered the apex of the water-sheds, declining East and West, although the head-waters of streams occasionally interlock. By a short "carry," one can pass from the head-waters of the Manistee to those of the Au Sable. I have seen marks on both of these streams that gave evidence that surveyors did so forty years ago, and have no doubt that it was a route used by the Indians in crossing from Lake Michigan to Lake Huron.

The country, except on the barrens, furnishes a fine growth of white and yellow pine, as well as oak, beech, maple, and other hard woods. White cedars—the arbor vitæ of the East—invariably fringe the banks of rivers a few miles below their sources, which are generally in ponds or lakes. These trees appear to love spring water, and do not appear until the stream has acquired that temperature. Growing on the banks of the streams, the current washes away the loose soil from their roots, which causes them to incline over

## The Michigan Grayling.

and at last to fall into the water; and these are called "sweepers." These rivers, from the constant influx of spring water, never freeze, and owing to the slight water-shed and sandy top-soil are not subject to freshets, a spring rise of two feet being considered excessive. Such streams, here and in Europe, are the home of the grayling, for it loves water of a low, even temperature and a smooth, steady current.

The game-laws of Michigan recently enacted forbid the spearing and netting of grayling at all times, and do not admit of them being taken even with hook and line from January until June. These fish acquire condition soon after spawning, but are better in autumn and in season nearly all winter. So after the first of September the sportsman can unite shooting with fishing. Several summers ago, in August, while running the Au Sable, we counted twelve deer and two bears. As they were out of season, and my friend Fitzhugh was a stickler for the observance of the game-laws in every instance, we resisted the temptation to shoot them.

The country I have described has, of course, none of that awe-inspiring scenery we find on the shores of Lake Superior; but with its clear, ever-flowing, ever-winding rivers over white and yellow sands, with graceful cedars projecting at a sharp angle from

*The "sweepers" characteristic of many Michigan streams were often a hazard to boatmen, a natural bridge for wildlife, and an attractive habitat for fish.*

the banks, and every bend of the stream opening a new view, it is novel and pleasing to one who has been shut up all winter in a crowded city. In running a grayling stream, the feeling is one of peace and quietude. There are no song-birds in those deep woods. One only hears the far-off falling of some old forest tree, or that weird sound caused by the rubbing of the branch of one tree against that of another, as they are swayed to and fro by the wind, and in the distance one can almost fancy that it is a human voice. Otherwise, all is as silent as death.

## The Michigan Grayling.

My first raid upon the grayling was in August, 1874, with Mr. Fitzhugh, of Bay City, on the Au Sable. We ran this river from Grayling, on the northern branch of the Jackson, Saginaw, and Lansing Railroad, to Thompson's, a distance of a hundred and sixty miles. From Thompson's, after loading our two boats on a stout two-horse wagon and occupying another with springs, we drove twenty-five miles to Tawas City, and then, after a few hours on a steamer, back to Bay City. There is no grayling-fishing at the station called Grayling, nor until one gets four or five miles down the stream where the cedars appear. From this as far as we ran it,—and there was yet sixty miles of it below Thompson's,—it is a beautiful stream, much prettier, I think, more rapid, and less obstructed with sweepers, than the Manistee. The distance by land is about seventy miles. On our second day, we killed and salted down—heads and tails off—a hundred and twenty pounds of fish, besides eating all we wanted. In one hanging rift close by the bank, as Len Iswel, my pusher, held on to the cedar boughs, I took at five casts fifteen fish, averaging three-quarters of a pound each. The following day, we fished along leisurely until we had our live-boxes, containing each sixty pounds, so full that the fish began to die. Then we passed over splendid pools in which we could see large schools of grayling on the bottom without casting a fly; for we would not destroy them in mere wantonness. In a few days, however, we came across occasional timber camps, when we commenced fishing again, and supplied all hands with fresh fish. One can leave Bay City by railroad in the morning and arrive at Grayling early enough in the afternoon to embark and drop down-stream seven or eight miles the same night. He should, however, engage boats and pushers beforehand.

There are two large branches, flowing almost as much as the main stream, that enter the Au Sable. The south-west comes in about forty-five miles below Grayling and the north branch sixty miles below. On this last stream there is a sluice dam, and when it is let off to float logs during the summer and autumn, the water is discolored somewhat, and the fish do not rise as well. One can get all the fishing he wants by running as far down as the south-west branch, which, as already stated, is forty-five miles by water, and is only twelve miles back to Grayling by land. He can engage a wagon at Grayling to come with ice on a stated day and haul back his boats, his luggage, and his fish, thus saving the labor of pushing back up-stream, which would occupy two days of incessant toil.

## The Michigan Grayling.

When I fished the Manistee several years ago, I went from Grayling with Mr. Fitzhugh and another friend, accompanied by our pushers, over "the barrens," a distance of eight miles, to a camp established by I. F. Babbit, to fish with hook and line for the Bay City and Detroit markets. We made a permanent camp four miles below Babbit's, and fished five days, giving him three-fourths of our fish, which he came for every day, and which (keeping none under a half pound) amounted to over five hundred pounds.

*Norris fished the Manistee when it was possible to catch hundreds of pounds of grayling in a few days; unfortunately most anglers killed almost all the fish they caught, often selling them locally.*

## Norris on Trout Fishing

One of my most pleasant trips, however, was that of the latter part of August and early in September of the following year, when, in company with two young friends, I spent two weeks on the Manistee. We went by the Grand Rapids and Indiana Railroad to Mancelona, well up toward the Straits of Mackinaw. Here we loaded boats, stores, and camp equipage on a wagon drawn by a pair of stout horses, and journeyed eleven miles east to the head-waters of the main branch. Our trip was dashed with a spice of adventure and a good deal of hard work. We had struck the stream higher up than we expected. It was small, scarcely sufficient to float our boats, and still had the temperature it had acquired in the little lake which was its source. There were no cedars, which only appear when the streams have flowed far enough from the ponds to feel the influence of spring water. On the morning of the second day, we came to the cedars and cold water, and with them the sweepers, which are cedars, as already described, which have been undermined by the current and have fallen into the water and always across the stream. We had three days and a half of hard chopping and hauling our boats over huge cedar logs, some of which had probably lain there for a century—for a cedar log, if it remains in the water, never rots. On coming to some

## The Michigan Grayling.

of these logs, we had to make a "carry," placing our luggage on their mossy covered trunks and pulling our empty boats over. We would then load up and go on to cut more sweepers and make more carries. At last, the stream widened and was free of sweepers, and we had magnificent fishing. The grayling were perfectly reckless and would take one's flies within ten feet of the boats. It was virgin water; no fly had heretofore been cast on it. After a day's sport, we came to the sweepers again, and had a day and a half more with them and half-sunken logs and a few carries. At two or three of these carries, the logs were over two feet through. Mosses had grown and spread on them until, as we saw by certain signs, bears used them as a highway. On one we found thrifty cedars growing at regular intervals from the parent trunk that were more than half a century old. Soon the stream increased so much in volume, and was so wide, that a tree falling across could not obstruct the passage of our boats; and finally we came to open water again. And so we ran the stream down to Walton Junction, a hundred and fifty miles by water, while it was scarce fifty on a bee-line.

The boat used on my first trip is worth description. It was built of white pine; bottom, 1 inch thick; sides, $5/8$; 16 feet long; 2.10 wide on top, 2.4 at bottom, and with a sheer of three inches on each side. The bottom was nearly level for eight feet in the center, with a sheer of five inches to the bow and seven inches to stern. The live-box was six feet from bow, extending back two feet. The sides were nailed to the bottom. Its weight was eighty pounds, and it carried two men—the angler and the pusher—with 200 pounds of luggage. With two coats of paint, it cost about fifteen dollars. The angler sits on the movable cover of the live-box, which is water-tight from other portions of the boat, and has holes bored in sides and bottom to admit of the circulation of the water to keep the fish alive, and as he captures his fish he slips them into holes on the right, and left sides. An axe was always taken along to clear the river of fallen logs and sweepers.

My customary tackle on these excursions is a twelve-foot rod of about eight and a half ounces; leaders eight feet long, and flies on hooks ranging from No. 7 to No. 10 (O'Shaughnessy). I have found most of the flies used on Pennsylvania streams effective, and one can scarcely go amiss in his selection. One summer, I used for two weeks the same whip, viz.: "Professor" for the stretcher, "Silver Widow" for first, and "White-winged Coachman" for second dropper. The first is tied with guinea-fowl feather for

## The Michigan Grayling.

wings, an amber or yellow-dyed hackle for legs, a yellow floss body wound with gold tinsel, and three sprigs of scarlet ibis for tail. The second has black wings, black hackle, and black body wound with silver tinsel. The third has white wings, red hackle, undyed, and body of peacock hurl.

As to stores. We found that for five men, including pushers, the following were about the right quantities for a two weeks' supply: 50 lbs. flour, 1 bushel potatoes, 25 lbs. of breakfast bacon, 12 lbs. butter, $1/2$ peck of onions, with corn meal, tea, coffee, sugar, condensed milk, a jar of pickles, and a few cans of corn and tomatoes. Bread is a difficult thing to take or to keep in good condition. I would advise, therefore, the taking of a portable sheetiron stove, which, with a baker and all other appliances and conveniences, does not weigh over thirty-five pounds. With a box of yeast powder, hot rolls can be had at every meal.

# CHAPTER FIVE

# *Fly-Fishing Alone.*

With many persons fishing is a mere recreation, a pleasant way of killing time. To the true angler, however, the sensation it produces is a deep unspoken joy, born of a longing for that which is quiet and peaceful, and fostered by an inbred love of communing with nature, as he walks through grassy meads, or listens to the music of the mountain torrent. This is why he loves occasionally—whatever may be his social propensity in-doors—to shun the habitations and usual haunts of men, and wander alone by the stream, casting his flies over its bright waters: or in his lone canoe to skim the unruffled surface of the inland lake, where no sound comes to his ear but the wild, flute-like cry of the loon, and where no human form is seen but his own, mirrored in the glassy water.

## Fly-Fishing Alone.

No wonder, then, that the fly-fisher loves at times to take a day, all by himself; for his very loneliness begets a comfortable feeling of independence and leisure, and a quiet assurance of resources within himself to meet all difficulties that may arise.

As he takes a near cut to the stream, along some blind road or cattle-path, he hears the wood-robin with its "to-whé," calling to its mate in the thicket, where itself was fledged the summer before. When he stops to rest at the "wind clearing," he recalls the traditionary stories told by the old lumbermen, of the Indians who occupied the country when their grandfathers moved out to the "back settlements," and, as he ruminates on the extinction, or silent removal of these children of the forest, he may think of the simple eloquent words of the chief to his companions, the last he uttered: "I will die, and you will go home to your people, and, as you go along, you will see the flowers, and hear the birds sing; but Pushmuttaha will see them and hear them no more; and when you come to your people they will say, 'Where is Pushmuttaha?' and you will say, 'He is dead:' then will your words come upon them, *like the falling of the great oak in the stillness of the woods."*

As he resumes his walk and crosses the little brook that "goes singing by," he remembers what he has read of the Turks, who built their bowers by the falling water, that they might be lulled by its music, as they smoked and dreamed of Paradise. But when the hoarse roar of the creek, where it surges against the base of the crag it has washed for ages, strikes his ear, or he hears it brawling over the big stones, his step quickens, and his pulse beats louder—he is no true angler if it does not—and he is not content until he gets a glimpse of its bright rushing waters at the foot of the hill.

Come forth, my little rod—"a better never did itself support upon" *an angler's arm,*—and let us rig up here on this pebbly shore! The rings are in a line, and now with this bit of waxed silk we take a few hitches backward and forward over the little wire loops which point in opposite directions at the ends of the ferules, to keep the joints from coming apart; for it would be no joke to throw the upper part of the rod out of the butt ferule, and have it sailing down some strong rift. The reel is on *underneath,* and not on top, as those Bass-fishers have it, who are always talking of Fire Island, Newport, and Narragansett Bay.

What shall my whip be? The water is full, I'll try a red hackle, its tail tipped with gold tinsel; for my dropper, I'll put on a good sized coachman with lead-colored wings, and as soon as I get a few handsful of grass, to throw in the bottom of my creel, I'll button on my landing-net and cross over, with the help of this stick of drift-wood, for it is pretty strong wading just here. Do you see that rift, and the flat rock at the lower end of it which just comes above the surface of the water, and divides the stream as it rushes into the pool below? There's fishing in rift and pool both; so I'll begin at the top of the rift, if I can get through these alders. Go in, my little rod, point foremost; I would not break that tip at this time to save the hair on my head;—hold! that twig has caught my dropper—easy, now,—all clear—through the bushes at last.

When I was here last July, and fished the pool below, there was no rift above, the water hardly came above my ankles; now it is knee-deep; if there was less it would be better for the pool; but it makes two casts now, where there was only one last summer, and I have no doubt there is a pretty fellow by the margin of the strong water, on this side of the rock,—an easy cast, too,—just about eight yards from the end of my tip. Not there—a little nearer the rock. What a swirl! He did not show more than his back; but he has my hackle. I had to strike him, too, for he took it under water like a bait—they will do so when the stream is full. Get out of that current, my hearty, and don't be flouncing on top, but keep underneath, and deport yourself like an honest, fair fighter! There you are, now, in slack water; you can't last long, tugging at this rate; so come along, to my landing-net; it's no use shaking your head at me! What a shame to thrust my thumb under that rosy gill! but there is no help for it, for you might give me the slip as I take the hook out of your mouth, and thrust you, tail-foremost, into the hole of my creel. You are my first fish, and you know you are my *luck*; so I would not lose you even if you were a little fellow of seven inches, instead of a good half-pound. I imbibed that superstition, not to throw away my first fish, when I was a boy, and have never got rid of it. Now, tumble about as much as you please; you have the whole basket to yourself.

## Fly-Fishing Alone.

Another cast—there ought to be more fish there. He rose short,—a little longer line—three feet more will do it—exactly so. Gently, my nine-incher! Take the spring of the rod for a minute or so—here you are! Once more, now. How the "young 'un" jumps! I'll throw it to him until he learns to catch; there, he has it. No use reeling in a chap of your size, but come along, hand-over-hand; I'll release you. Go, now, and don't rise at a fly again until you are over nine inches.

Not a fly on the water! So I have nothing to imitate, even if imitation were necessary. Take care! that loose stone almost threw me. I'll work my way across the current, and get under the lee of that boulder, and try each side of the rift where it runs into the pool below the flat rock. Not a fish in the slack water on this side; they are looking for grub and larvæ in the rift. Now, how would you like my coachman, by way of a change of diet? There's a chance for you— try it. Bosh! he missed it; but he is not pricked. Once more. Oh, ho! is it there you are, my beauty? Don't tear that dropper off. Hold him tight, O'Shaughnessy; you are the greatest hook ever invented. How he runs the line out, and plays off into the swift water! It would be rash to check him now; but give him a few feet, and edge him over to the side of the rift where there is slack water. That's better; now tug away, while I recover some of my line. You are off into the current again, are you? but not so wicked. The click on this reel is too weak, by half—he gives in now, and is coming along, like an amiable, docile fish, as he is. Whiz! why, what's the matter, now? Has "the devil kicked him on end?" as my friend with the "tarry breeks" has it. He has taken but two or three yards of line, though. How he hugs the bottom, and keeps the main channel! Well, he can't last much longer. Here he comes now, with a heavy drag, and a distressing strain on my middle joint; and now I see him dimly, as I get him into the eddy; but there's something tugging at the tail-fly. Yes, I have a brace of them, and that accounts for the last dash, and the stubborn groping for the bottom. What a clever way of trolling to get an obliging Trout to take your dropper, and go sailing around with four feet of gut, and a handsome stretcher at the end of it, setting all the fish in the pool crazy, until some unlucky fellow hooks himself in the side of his mouth. How shall I get the pair into my basket? There is no way but reeling close up, and getting the lower one unto my net first, and then with another dip to secure the fish on the dropper; but it must be done gently. So—well done; three-quarters of a pound to be credited to the dropper, and a half-pound to the stretcher—total, one pound and a quarter. That will do for the present. So I'll sit down on that flat rock and light my dudeen, and try the remainder of the water presently. I'll not compromise for less than four half-pound fish before I leave the pool.

These are *some* of the incidents that the lone fly-fisher experiences on a favorable day, and the dreams and anticipations he has indulged in through the long gloomy winter are in part realized. "Real joy," some one has said, is "a serious thing," and the solitary angler proves it conclusively to himself. He is not troubled that some ardent young brother of the rod may fish ahead of him, and disturb the water without availing himself of all the chances; or that a more discreet companion may pass by some of the pools and riffs without bestowing the attention on them they deserve; but in perfect quietude, and confidence in his ability to meet every contingency that may occur, he patiently and leisurely tries all the places that offer fair. What if he does get hung up in a projecting branch of some old elm, that leans over the water? he does not swear and jerk his line away, and leave his flies dangling there—it is a difficulty that will bring into play his ingenuity, and perhaps his dexterity in climbing, and he sets about recover-

## Norris on Trout Fishing

ing his flies with the same patient steadiness of purpose that Cæsar did in building his bridge, or that possessed Bonaparte in crossing the Alps, and feels as much satisfaction as either of those great generals, in accomplishing his ends.

If he takes "an extraordinary risk," as underwriters call it, in casting under boughs that hang within a few feet of the water, on the opposite side of some unwadeable rift or pool, and his stretcher should fasten itself in a tough twig, or his dropper grasp the stem of an obstinate leaf, he does not give it up in despair, or, consoling himself with the idea that he has plenty of flies and leaders in his book, pull away and leave his pet spinner and some favorite hackle to hang there as a memento of his temerity in casting so near the bushes. Far from it; he draws sufficient line off his reel and through the rings to give slack enough to lay his rod down, marking well where his flies have caught, and finds some place above or below where he can cross; then by twisting with a forked stick, or drawing in the limb with a hooked one, he releases his leader, and throws it clear off into the water, that he may regain it when he returns to his rod, and reels in his line; or he cuts it off and lay it carefully in his fly-book, and then recrosses the river. A fig for the clearing-ring and rod-scythe and all such cockney contrivances, he never cumbers his pockets with them. Suppose he does break his rod—he sits patiently down and splices it. If the fracture is a compound one, and it would shorten the piece too much to splice it, he resorts to a sailor's device, and *fishes the stick,* by binding a couple of flat pieces of hard wood on each side.

Captain Marryatt, in one of his books, says, a man's whole lifetime is spent in getting into scrapes and getting out of them. This is very much the case with the fly-fisher, and he should always curb any feeling of haste or undue excitement, remembering at such times, that if he loses his temper he is apt to lose his fish, and sometimes his tackle also.

My neighbor asked me once if Trout-fishing was not a very unhealthy amusement—he thought a man must frequently have damp feet. Well, it is, I answered; but if he gets wet up to his middle at the outset, and has reasonable luck, there is no healthier recreation.———But I have sat here long enough. I'll fill my pipe again and try the head of that swift water—If this confounded war lasts a year longer "Lynchburg" will go up to three dollars a pound, but it will be cheap then compared with those soaked and drugged segars that are imposed upon us for the "Simon-Pure," under so many captivating names. At all events *this* is what it professes to be, good homely tobac——— Whe-e-euh! What a dash! and how strong and steady he pulls; some old fellow "with moss on his back," from under that log, no doubt of it. Is it line you want?—take it, eight—ten—fifteen feet—but no more if you please. How he keeps the middle of the rift! Don't tell me about the "grace of the curve," and all that sort of thing; if the bend of this rod isn't the line of beauty I never saw it before, except of course in the outline of a woman's drapery. Speaking of lines, I'll get a little of this in as I lead the fellow down stream, even at the risk of disturbing the swim below. It is the best plan with a large fish; I have Sir Humphrey Davy's authority for it, although I believe with Fisher, of the "Angler's Souvenir," that he was more of a philosopher than an angler. Talk of "dressing for dinner," when the fish are rising! Steady and slow, my boy, you are giving in at last—two pounds and a half or not an ounce! now I see you "as through a glass, darkly"—a little nearer, my beauty— Bah! what a fool I am! here a fish of a half-pound has hooked himself amidship, and of course offering five times the resistance he would if fairly hooked in the mouth, and no damage to his breathing apparatus while fighting, either; for he keeps his wind all the while. If he had been regularly harnessed, he could

*Fly-Fishing Alone.*

not have pulled with more advantage to himself and greater danger to my tackle in this rough water. I thought I had been deceived in this way often enough to know when a fish was hooked foul.

Now I call it strong wading coming down through that dark ravine; I must take a rest and put on a fresh dropper. And so my friend asked me if it was not very lonesome, fishing by myself. Why these little people of the woods are much better company than folks who continually bore you with the weather, and the state of their stomachs or livers, and what they ate for breakfast, or the price of gold, or the stock-market, when you have forgotten whether you have a liver or not, and don't care the toss of a penny what the price of gold is; or whether "Reading" is up or down. Lonesome!—It was only just now the red squirrel came down the limb of that birch, whisking his bushy tail, and chattering almost in my face. The mink, as he snuffed the fish-tainted air from my old creel, came out from his hole amongst the rocks and ran along within a few feet of me. Did he take my old coat to be a part of this rock, covered with lichens and gray mosses? I recollect once in the dim twilight of evening, a doe with her fawns came down to the stream to drink; I had the wind of her, and could see into her great motherly eyes as she raised her head. A moment since the noisy king-fisher poised himself on the dead branch of the hemlock, over my left shoulder, as if he would peep into the hole of my fish-basket. The little warbler sang in the alders close by my old felt hat, as if he would burst his swelling throat with his loud glad song. Did either of them know that I am of a race whose first impulse is to throw a stone or shoot a gun at them? And the sparrow-hawk on that leafless spray extending over the water, sitting there as grave and dignified as a bank president when you ask him for a discount; is he aware that I can tap him on the head with the tip of my rod?—These are some of the simple incidents on the stream, which afterwards awaken memories,

> "That like voices from afar off
> Call to us to pause and listen,
> Speak in tones so plain and childlike,
> Scarcely can the ear distinguish
> Whether they are sung or spoken."

But I must start for the open water below— What a glorious haze there is just now, and how demurely the world's great eye peeps through it! Trout are not very shy though, before the middle of

## Fly-Fishing Alone.

May, even when the sun is bright. I have sometimes taken my best fish at high noon, at this season of the year.—I am as hungry as a horsefly, though it is only "a wee short hour ayont the twal." So I'll unsling my creel by that big sycamore, and build my fire in the hollow of it. If I burn it down there will be no action for trespass in a wooden country like this.

What boys are those crossing the foot-log? I'll press them into my service for awhile, and make them bring wood for my fire. I know them now; the larger one has cause to remember me "with tears of gratitude," for I bestowed on him last summer a score of old flies, a used-up leader, and a limp old rod. He offered me the liberal sum of two shillings for the very implement I have in my hand now; and to buy three flies from me *at four cents apiece.*—Halloo, Paul! what have you done with the rod I gave you—caught many Trout with it this season? Come over the creek, you and your brother, and get me some dry wood, and gather a handful or two of the furze from that old birch to light it with. I'll give you a pair of flies—real gay ones.

Dining *alone* may be counted almost the only drawback to one's taking a day to himself, and you are glad of any stray native who is attracted by the smoke of your fire. Your whiskey is beyond a perad-

## Norris on Trout Fishing

*Norris recommended that when fishing in unfamiliar country it was wise to be kind to the local boys, because "stones are of very convenient size along the creek to throw at a surly fisherman."*

venture, better than he has in his cupboard at home; he is invariably out of tobacco—a chew or a pipeful, and a swig at your flask, will make him communicative. If he has not already dined, he will readily accept a roasted Trout and a piece of bread and butter, and while eating will post you as to all the Trout-streams within ten miles. It is, therefore, a matter of policy to cultivate the good feeling of the natives, the boys especially, as stones are of very convenient size along the creek to throw at a surly fisherman. A few of "Conroy's journal-flies," which have occupied the back leaves of your fly-book for long years are profitable things to invest in this way, for three boys out of four you meet with, will ask you to sell them "a pair of fly-hooks," which of course results in your giving them a brace or so that are a little the worse for wear, or too gay for your own use.

If the fly-fisher, though, would have "society where none intrudes," or society that *won't* intrude, let him take a lad of ten or twelve along to carry his dinner, and to relieve him after the roast, by transferring part of the contents of his creel to the empty dinner-basket. The garrulity and queer questions of a country boy of this age are amusing, when you are disposed to talk. Any person who has sojourned at my friend Jim Henry's, and had his good-natured untiring boy Luther for his *gilly*, will acknowledge the advantage of such a "tail" even if it has not as many joints as a Highland laird's.

If there *is* an objection to a Trout-roast, it is that a man eats too much, and feels lazy after dinner. But what of that? it is a luxurious indolence, without care for the morrow—Care! why, he left that at home when he bought his railroad ticket, and shook off the dust of the city from his hobnailed boots.

What pretty bright Trout there are in this bold rocky creek! it would be called a river in England, and so it is. We Americans have an ugly way of calling every stream not a hundred yards wide, a creek. It is all well enough when the name is applied to some still sedgy water, which loses half of its depth, and three-fourths of its width, at low tide, and is bankfull on the flood. But speckled fellows like these don't live there. De Kay must have received some inspiration at a Trout-roast, when he gave them the specific name of "Fontinalis," and they are truly the Salmon of the fountain; for a stream like this and its little tributaries, whose fountains are everywhere amongst these rugged hills, are their proper home. What an ignorant fellow Poietes was to ask Halieus if the red spots on a Trout were not "marks of disease—a hectic kind of beauty?" Any boy along the creek knows better. And what a pedantic old theorist Sir Humphrey was, to tell him that the absence of these spots was a sign of high condition. Well, it may be in England, for the river Trout there, are a different species from ours. But I'll bet my old rod against a bob-fly that there is twice as much pluck and dash in our little fellows with the "hectic" spots. I don't wonder that Trout like these so inspired Mr. Barnwell, who wrote the "Game Fish of the North," when, with his fancy in high feather, he mounted his Pegasus and went off—"How splendid is the sport to deftly throw the long line and small fly, with the pliant single-handed rod, and with eye and nerve on the strain, to watch the loveliest darling of the wave, the spotted naiad, dart from her mossy bed, leap high into the air, carrying the strange deception in her mouth, and, turning in her flight, plunge back to her crystal home."

Julius Cæsar! what "high-flying" Trout this gentleman must have met with in his time. Now, I never saw a Trout "dart from her mossy bed," because I never found Trout to lie on a bed of that sort; nor "leap high into the air, and turning in her flight plunge back," as a fish-hawk does. In fact, I may safely say I never saw a Trout *soar* more than eight or ten inches above its "crystal home." I honor "Barnwell" for the Anglomania which has seized him—he has been inoculated with a good scab, and the virus has penetrated his system: but I can't help being reminded by his description, of the eloquence of a member of a country debating society in Kentucky, who commenced—"Happiness, Mr. President, is like a crow situated on some far-distant mountain, which the eager sportsman endeavors in vain to no purpose to reproach." And concluded—"The poor man, Mr. President, reclines beneath the shade of some widespreading and umbrageous tree, and calling his wife and the rest of his little children around him, bids their thoughts inspire to scenes beyond the skies. He views Neptune, Plato, Venus, and Jupiter, the Lost Pleides, the Auroly Bolyallis, and other fixed stars, which it was the lot of the immorral Newton first to depreciate and then to deplore."

But a gray-headed man who cannot tie a decent knot in his casting-line without the aid of his spectacles, should forget such nonsense. There is one consolation, however, that this "decay of natur," which brings with it the necessity for glasses in seeing small objects within arm's length, gives in like ratio, the power of seeing one's flies at a distance on the water; there was old Uncle Peter Stewart who could knock a pheasant's head off at fifty yards with his rifle, and see a gnat across the Beaverkill, when he was past sixty. Here is the sun shining as bright now as if he had not blinked at noon, and such weather, not too hot and not too cold; I must acknowledge, though, my teeth *did* chatter this morning when I waded across at the ford.

*Fly-Fishing Alone.*

> "Sweet day, so cool, so calm, so bright,
> The bridal of the earth and sky;
> The dew shall weep thy fall to night,
>             For thou must die."

I'll start in here, for it appears there is always luck in the pool or rift under the lee of the smoke where one cooks his Trout. It is strange, too, for it seems natural that the smoke would drive the flies away, and as a consequence the fish get out of the notion of rising. But no matter, here goes. Just as I supposed, and a brace of them at the first cast. Come ashore on the sloping gravel, my lively little fellows,—eight and nine inches—the very size for the pan; but who wants to eat fried Trout after cooking them under the ashes or on a forked stick?

There are no good fish here; the water is not much more than knee-deep, and they have no harbor amongst those small pebble-stones. I have thrown in a dozen little fellows within the last ten minutes. I'll go to the tail of that strong rift below the saw-mill. The last time I fished it was when that lean hungry-looking Scotchman came over here from Jim Henry's; he had been sneaking through the bushes and poaching all the little brooks around, where the fish had run up to spawn, with his confounded worm-bait. This stream was low then and the fish shy; I had approached the end of the rift carefully and was trying to raise them at long cast in the deep water, when he—without even saying "by your leave"—waded in within a few yards of where they were rising, and splashed his buck-shot sinker and wad of worms right amongst them. I said nothing, and he did not appear to think that interfering with my sport so rudely was any breach of good manners, or of the rules of fair fishing. A Scotchman, to catch Trout with a *worm*! Poor fellow! his piscatory education must have been neglected, or he belonged to that school who brag *only* on numbers. I know a party of that sort who come up here every summer from Easton and bring a *sauer-kraut stanner* to pack their Trout in, and salt down all they take without eating one, until they get home. They catch all they can and keep *all* they catch, great and small. Bah! a poor little *salted* Trout—it tastes more like a piece of "yaller soap" than a fish. Such fishermen are but one remove from the bark peelers I found snaring and netting Trout in the still water below here, last August. I can just see their shanty from here. "Instruments of cruelty are in their habitations. O my soul, come not thou into their secret; unto their assembly, mine honor, be not thou united!"

There is the sawyer's dog; if he comes much nearer I'll psychologize him with one of these "dunnicks"! But he turns tail as soon as I stoop to pick one up. Now for it—just at the end of the swift water—ah! my beauty—fifteen inches, by all that is lovely! He threw his whole length out of water—try it again—I can't raise him. This won't do. Am I cold, or am I nervous, that I should shake like a palsied old man because I missed that fish? Fie on you, Mr. Nestor, you who have run the rapids at the "Rough Waters" on the Nipissiguit, in a birch canoe, with a Salmon at the end of sixty yards of line, and your pipe in your mouth; I thought you had gotten past a weakness of this kind. But it will only make bad worse, and convince that Trout of the cheat to throw over him again; so I must leave him now, and get back to the log on that sunny bank and compose myself with a few whiffs, while I change my flies. It will be just fifteen minutes until I knock the ashes out of my pipe; by that time my vaulting friend will likely forget the counterfeit I tried to impose on him, if I offer him something else.

Now Dick gave me this for a meershaum, and I have no doubt Mr. Doll sold it for one in good faith;

*Norris and many of his angling companions were so fond of their pipes and cigars that Norris proclaimed it a pity that infants are not taught to smoke.*

but it is a very "pale complected" pipe for one of that family. I have smoked it steadily for a year, and there is only the slightest possible tinge of orange about the root of the stem. It is hardly as dark as this ginger hackle in my hat-band. However, it is light, and carries a big charge for a pipe of its size, and the shortness of the stem brings the smoke so comfortably under the nose—a great desideratum in the open air. The pipe must have been instituted expressly for the fisherman; it is company when he is lonesome, and never talks when he wants to be quiet; it concentrates his ideas and assists his judgment when he discusses any important matter with himself, such as the selection of a killing stretcher. No wonder the Indians smoked at their council-fires; and, as for the nerves, put it against Mrs. Winslow's soothing syrup. What a pity it is that infants are not taught to smoke! What shall my stretcher be; that fish refused Hofland's Fancy; now let me try one of my own fancy. Here is something a great deal prettier; a purple body in place of a snuff-brown, and light wings from a lead-colored pigeon instead of a sober woodcock feather. What a pretty fly—half sad, half gay in its attire, like an interesting young widow, when she decides on shedding her weeds, and "begins to take notice." I'll change my dropper also—here it is; body of copper-colored peacock hurl, wings of the feather of an old brown hen, mottled with yellow specks. What a plain homely look it has; it reminds me of "the Girl with the Calico Dress." You are not as showy, my dear miss, as the charming little widow, but certain individuals of my acquaintance are quite conscious of your worth. Let me see which of you will prove most attractive to my speckled friend. So here goes—two to one on the widow—lost, by jingo! He looked at her and sailed slowly away. Has he ever heard of the warning that the sage Mr. Weller gave his son "Samivel?" Perhaps, then, he will take a notion to "the girl with the calico dress." Once more—now do take care! Ah ha! my old boy, you would be indiscreet, after all, and the widow has victimized you. Now she'll lead you a dance! Don't be travelling off with her as if you were on your wedding tour, for I know you would like to get rid of her already; but there is no divorce beneath the water,—you are mine, says she, "until death us do part!"

There you are, now! the three-minutes' fight has completely taken the wind out of you. That's the last flap of your tail; the widow has killed you "as dead as a mackerel." Acting the gay Lothario, were you? I know some scaly old fellows who play the same game ashore, stealthily patronizing Mrs. Allen, subsidizing the tailor, bootmaker, dentist, and barber, and slyly endeavoring to take off a discount of twenty-five per cent. from old Father Time's bill. But that won't do, for folks of any discernment know at a glance those spavined, short-winded, shaky old fellows, who trot themselves out, as if they were done-up for the horse-market. Lie there, my Turveydrop, until I move down a little, and try under the bushes, on the opposite side.

With this length of line I can just come close enough to the alders to miss them. Dance lightly, O my brown girl, and follow in her wake, dear widow, as I draw you hitherward. Ah, ha! and so it is; there is one dashing fellow who sees charms in your homely dress. How he vaults!—nine rails, and a top rail! Did you ever know Turner Ashby? Not Beau Turner—I mean Black Turner. Did he ever straddle a bit of horse-flesh with more mettle? None of your Conestogas. There he goes again! How long have you belonged to the circus? But he can't run all day at that gait; he begins to flag, at last, and here he is now, coming in on the "quarter stretch." There you are, at last—died as game as a Dominica chicken. Once more, now. I knew it.—And again.

Three times my brace of beauties have come tripping home across the deep whirling rapid, and three bright Trout lie on the gravel behind me. I begin at last to long for the sound of some friendly voice, and the sight of a good-humored face. I must keep my appointment with Walter at the foot-bridge; so I am off. Some of the "Houseless" don't like this solitary sport. I know one of them who would as soon be guilty of drinking alone; but *he* is not a contemplative angler, and has never realized how hungry some folks get through the winter for a little fishing. Maybe he has never read what William Howitt says, in his "Rural Life in England," about fishing alone. It will come home to every quiet fly-fisher. See what an unveiling of the heart it is, when the angler is alone with God and Nature.

"People that have not been innoculated with the true spirit may wonder at the infatuation of anglers—but true anglers leave them very contentedly to their wondering, and follow their diversions with a keen delight. Many old men there are of this class that have in them a world of science—not science of the book, or of regular tuition, but the science of actual experience. Science that lives, and will die with them; except it be dropped out piecemeal, and with the gravity becoming its importance, to some young neophyte who has won their good graces by his devotion to their beloved craft. All the mysteries of times and seasons, of baits, flies of every shape and hue; worms, gentles, beetles, compositions, or substances found by proof to possess singular charms. These are a possession which they hold with pride, and do not hold in vain. After a close day in the shop or factory, what a luxury is a fine summer evening to one of these men, following some rapid stream, or seated on a green bank, deep in grass and flowers, pulling out the spotted Trout, or resolutely but subtilely bringing some huge Pike or fair Grayling from its lurking place beneath the broad stump and spreading boughs of the alder. Or a day, a summer's day, to such a man, by the Dove or the Wye, amid the pleasant Derbyshire hills; by Yorkshire or Northumbrian stream; by Trent or Tweed; or the banks of Yarrow; by Teith or Leven, with the glorious hills and heaths of Scotland around him. Why, such a day to such a man, has in it a life and spirit of enjoyment to which the feelings of cities and palaces are dim. The heart of such a man—the power and passion of deep felicity that come breathing from mountains and moorlands; from clouds that sail above, and storms blustering and growling in the wind; from all the mighty magnificence, the solitude and antiquity of Nature upon him—Ebenezer Elliott only can unfold. The weight of the poor man's life—

the cares of poverty—the striving of huge cities, visit him as he sits by the beautiful stream—beautiful as a dream of eternity, and translucent as the everlasting canopy of heaven above him;—they come, but he casts them off for the time, with the power of one who feels himself strong in the kindred spirit of all things around; strong in the knowledge that he is a man; an immortal—a child and pupil in the world-school of the Almighty. For that day he is more than a king—he has the heart of humanity, and faith and spirit of a saint. It is not the rod and line that floats before him—it is not the flowing water, or the captured prey that he perceives in those moments of admission to the heart of nature, so much as the law of the testimony of love and goodness written on everything around him with the pencil of Divine beauty. He is no longer the wearied and oppressed—the trodden and despised—walking in threadbare garments amid men, who scarcely deign to look upon him as a brother man—but he is reassured and recognised to himself in his own soul, as one of those puzzling, aspiring, and mysterious existences for whom all this splendid world was built, and for whom eternity opens its expecting gates. These are magnificent speculations for a poor, angling carpenter or weaver; but Ebenezer Elliott can tell us that they are his legitimate thoughts, when he can break for an instant the bonds of his toiling age, and escape to the open fields. Let us leave him dipping his line in the waters of refreshing thought."

Thus writes William Howitt. But there is the foot-bridge, and here are my little friends, the Sand-pipers. How often the fly-fisher sees them running along the pebbly margin of the Trout stream (as Wilson truly says), "continually nodding their heads;" sometimes starting with their peculiar short shrill note, from their nests in the wave-washed tufts of long grass, flapping along the creek sideways, as if wounded in leg or wing, to decoy the fancied destroyer from the nest of downy little snipelings. And there, where the waters of the noisy rapid finds rest in the broad shallow below, is one perched on a big gray boulder, as gray as herself. How lonely she seems there, like the last of her race, were it not that her constant mate is on the strand below, busily engaged picking up larva and seedling muscles for its little ones in the nest up the creek.

# CHAPTER SIX

# *The Great Lake Trout.*

*Salmo naymacush:* Richardson.

The *Naymacush* can scarcely be enumerated amonst what are strictly called "sporting fish;" but as it possesses several points of interest to the angler, besides its enormous size, a work of so general a character as this would be incomplete without a notice of this monster Trout. It is purely a fresh-water fish, and exceeds in size any species of Salmon known. Its average weight is nearly double that of the true Salmon. In the waters of the United States, it is found in Lakes Superior, Michigan, Huron, and Erie; the Falls of Niagara preventing its passage into Lake Ontario.

Dr. Richardson describes this fish under the above scientific name, giving it the Indian appellation, and says it is found in Winter Lake. I have no doubt it also inhabits Winnipeg, Athabasca, Great Slave, Great Bear, and other lakes which discharge their waters into Hudson's Bay and the Arctic Ocean. With us they are most abundant in Lake Superior, though they are taken in quantities in Lakes Huron, Erie, and Michigan. They are generally caught in gill-nets sunk at the bottom, on set lines, and by fishing with hand-lines in deep water, as well as by trolling at certain seasons of the year. In winter they are taken by spearing through a hole in the ice.

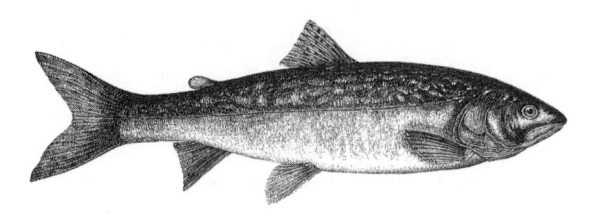

In stopping for a few days at Mackinaw some years ago, I saw a Trout of this species weighing forty pounds. It was taken on a set line in the straits opposite Bois Blanc Island. The fisherman assured me it was not a very unusual size. Its proportions were rather shorter than those indicated by the preceding engraving. It has been taken in Lake Superior weighing as much as a hundred pounds. The flavor of this fish is nothing to boast of. They are seldom eaten when the delicate Whitefish, which inhabits the same waters, is on the table.

It is said that the *Naymacush* spawns along the shores of the lakes in the month of November. I have never been able to ascertain whether they seek those places where the aerated waters of brooks or rivers flow into the lake, or that they enter the mouths of such streams for that purpose. They are doubtless fish of rapid growth, although there is no reliable means of judging what size they attain in a given time.

In returning from Sault Ste. Marie in July, 1844, in a "Mackinaw boat," such as was then in general use among the voyageurs, I threw a line over, with two stout 00 Kirby hooks at the end of it, baited with a white rag and a piece of my red flannel shirt, and hooked several Trout of this kind near the "Detour," but the hooks in every instance but one were straightened or broken, and the fish lost; the single exception being a small one of about eight pounds, which was evidently a young fish, from the fact of its meat cutting nearly white, when we broiled it.

The degree of skill attained by the Indians, half-breeds, and traders in spearing the *Naymacush* is wonderful; but it is only by early education, or long practice, that they become adepts at the art. The usual mode is as follows:—

The spearer provides himself with the necessary weapon fastened into the end of a long ash handle, and the leaden counterfeit of a small fish, six or seven inches long, which he keeps bright by scraping with a knife, and ties it, evenly balanced, with a string, which passes through a small hole in the back. After making a hole of proper size in the ice for spearing and taking out his captives, he cuts another, through which he lowers the leaden imitation; then covering the larger hole and himself by means of one or more blankets suspended on upright sticks, he is ready for operation, and proceeds to lower and raise the counterfeit fish to lure the great Trout within reach of his spear. As the large hole is darkened by the blankets, the spearer is not seen by the Trout below; as he rises in pursuit of the leaden fish and comes within striking distance, he is impaled by the deadly spear and landed on the ice, where, after a few flaps of his tail, he dies a martyr to his voracity and curiosity.

The wood-cut of this fish I have taken from Mr. E. Cabot's representation, filling in the proportions somewhat between the anal and caudal fins to suit my own notions of its form.

# CHAPTER SEVEN

# *A Note on Fly Theory.*

Much, perhaps most, of the theoretical knowledge of flies acquired by the reading angler, when he begins, is obtained from the writings of our brethren of the "Fast-anchored Isle." Every fly-fisher can read Chitty, Ronalds, Rene, "Ephemera," and others, with interest and profit. Though I do not pretend to condemn or think lightly of their precepts, drawn from long experience of bright waters and its inmates, yet if followed without modification and proper allowance for climate, season, water, and insect life here as contrasted with England, the beginner is apt to be led into many errors, corrected only by long summers of experience. So he will come at last to the conclusion, that of the many flies described and illustrated in English books, or exhibited on the fly-maker's pattern-cards, a very limited assortment is really necessary, and many totally useless, in making up his book. He will also find, after the lapse of some years, that of the great variety with which he at first stored his book, he has gradually got rid of at least three-fourths of them, as he has of the theory of strict imitation, and the routine system (that is, an exact imitation of the natural fly, and particular flies for each month), and settles down to the use of a half dozen or so of hackles and a few winged flies; and with such assortment, considers his book stocked beyond any contingency.

An extensive knowledge of flies and their names can hardly be of much practical advantage. Many a rustic adept is ignorant of a book ever having been written on fly-fishing, and knows the few flies he uses only by his own limited vocabulary. One of the most accomplished fly-fishers I ever met with has told me that his first essay was with the scalp of a red-headed woodpecker tied to the top of his hook. Notwithstanding all this, there is still a harmonious blending of colors or attractive hues, as well as the neat and graceful tying of a fly, that makes it killing.

# ADDITIONAL READINGS ON THADDEUS NORRIS

Norris has been discussed and eulogized in many angling books and in the usual biographical dictionaries. The following short list is a good start, and will provide references to many other sources of information.

Arnold Gingrich, *The Joys of Trout*. New York: Crown, 1973, 162–165.

Arnold Gingrich, *The Fishing in Print*. New York: Winchester Press, 1974, 150–197.

Jerry Girard, "Thaddeus Norris Jr.: America's Greatest Fly-Fisherman, *The Art of Angling Journal* 2(1), 2003, 8–19.

Charles Goodspeed, *Angling in America*, Boston: Houghton Mifflin, 1939, 219–224.

"Joe" (Joseph Townsend), "In Memoriam," *Forest and Stream*, April 26, 1877, 182.

# SOURCES OF THE CHAPTERS

One: "Angling," Thaddeus Norris, *The American Angler's Book*. Philadelphia: E. H. Butler, 1865, 27–36.

Two: "Brook Trout. Speckled Brook Trout," Thaddeus Norris, *The American Angler's Book*. Philadelphia: E. H. Butler, 1865, 194–205.

Three: "Trout Fly-Fishing.—The Stream," Thaddeus Norris, *The American Angler's Book*. Philadelphia: E. H. Butler, 1865, 327–42.

Four: "The Michigan Grayling," in Alfred M. Mayer, editor, *Sport with Gun and Rod in American Woods and Waters*. New York: The Century Company, 1883, 493–506. This chapter previously appeared in periodical form, but the book chapter was chosen for use here because it was, presumably, the author's final preferred version.

Five: "Fly-Fishing Alone," Thaddeus Norris, *The American Angler's Book*. Philadelphia: E. H. Butler, 1865, 567–86.

Six: "The Great Lake Trout," Thaddeus Norris, *The American Angler's Book*. Philadelphia: E. H. Butler, 1865, 250–54.

Seven: "A Note on Fly Theory," Thaddeus Norris, *The American Angler's Book*. Philadelphia: E. H. Butler, 1865, 313–14.

## ALSO IN THE SERIES

*Theodore Gordon is one of American angling's freshest and most original voices, and his trout-fishing tales and lessons are rich with the adventure and awe that come from a lifetime of inspired engagement with nature.*

*Theodore Gordon on Trout*
*$16.95, hardcover, 4 x 6, 160 pages, 27 b/w illustrations*

## ALSO IN THE SERIES

*Frederic Halford's writings launched the dry-fly revolution and have influenced every generation of serious fly fishers since. He was a gifted naturalist who witnessed an historic moment in the development of fly fishing.*

*Halford on the Dry Fly*
$16.95, hardcover, 4 x 6, 160 pages,
11 b/w illustrations

*G. E. M. Skues has been described not only as the father of nymph fishing, but as the greatest fly fisher who ever lived. His books established him as a masterful angling theorist.*

*Skues on Trout*
$16.95, hardcover, 4 x 6, 160 pages,
7 b/w illustrations